THE ULTIMATE
BREAD MACHINE
COOKBOOK

THE ULTIMATE
BREAD MACHINE
COOKBOOK

FAMILY RECIPES FOR
FOOLPROOF, DELICIOUS BAKES

TIFFANY DAHLE

Author and Founder of Peanut Blossom

PAGE STREET
PUBLISHING CO.

PAGE STREET
PUBLISHING CO.

Copyright © 2021 Tiffany Dahle

First published in 2021 by

Page Street Publishing Co.

27 Congress Street, Suite 105

Salem, MA 01970

www.pagestreetpublishing.com

Distributed by Macmillan, sales in Canada by The Canadian Manda Group.

25 24 23 22 21   1 2 3 4 5

ISBN-13: 978-1-64567-446-7

ISBN-10: 1-64567-446-0

Library of Congress Control Number: 2021931373

Cover and book design by Laura Benton for Page Street Publishing Co.

Photography by Tiffany Dahle

Printed and bound in China

For my husband, Tim, who made me do it.

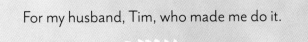

"You are the butter to my bread and the breath to my life."
–Paul to Julia Child, *Julie & Julia*

CONTENTS

Introduction 9

The Quick Start Guide 10

CHAPTER 1
CLASSIC BAKERY ESSENTIALS 15

Milk & Honey Bread 17

Brown Sugar Oatmeal Bread 18

Honey Whole Wheat Bread 21

Cinnamon Raisin Bread 22

Italian Bread 25

Caraway Rye Bread 26

Steakhouse Brown Bread 29

Everything Bagel Bread 30

Speedy Sourdough Loaf 33

Sourdough Pesto Swirl 34

CHAPTER 2
SOUP & SANDWICH PARTNERS 37

Rosemary Herb Bread 39

Farmers' Market Veggie Patch Bread 40

Savory Swiss & Onion Bread 43

Savory Sweet Potato Bread 44

Cucumber Dill Tzatziki Bread 47

Sun-Dried Tomato Parmesan Bread 48

Loaded Baked Potato Bread 51

Honeyed Blue Cheese Bread 52

Beer Flight Bread 55

Jalapeño Popper Cornbread 56

CHAPTER 3
BREAKFAST TABLE TREATS 59

Brioche 61

Lemon Blueberry Bread 62

The Best Banana Bread 65

Maple Pecan Bread 66

Blueberry Streusel Muffin Bread 69

Apple Crisp Bread 71

Aloha Pineapple Bread 75

Chocolate Almond Bread 77

Orange Chocolate Chip Bread 81

Almond Cherry Bread 82

CHAPTER 4
HOLIDAY CELEBRATIONS 85

Warm & Cozy Pumpkin Bread 87

Hot Buttered Rum Bread 88

Savory Stuffing Bread 91

Spiced Eggnog & Pear Bread 92

Cranberry & White Chocolate Delight 95

It's Not a Fruitcake Bread 97

Classic Hummingbird Bread   101

Sweet Carrot Cake Bread   103

Poppy Seed Tea Bread   107

Luck of the Irish Soda Bread   108

CHAPTER 5

FUN WITH DOUGH   111

How to Bake a Traditional Loaf in Your Oven   112

Hot Cross Buns   115

Buttery Dinner Rolls   118

Garlic Pull-Apart Bread   121

Classic Cinnamon Rolls   123

Fluffy Focaccia   127

Classic Pretzel Twists   128

Epic Party Pretzel Platter   133

Tim's Buns   137

Strawberry Cream Cheese Swirls   138

Caramel Pecan Breakfast Buns   141

CHAPTER 6

HOW DOES THIS THING
WORK EXACTLY?   144

Common Questions from Newbie
Bread Bakers   145

You Are Smarter Than Your Machine   149

The Essential Way to Add Ingredients to
Your Bread Pan   150

How to Use a Food Scale to Make Perfectly
Consistent Breads Every Time   151

How to Assemble a Layered Dough in
Your Bread Machine   151

Getting Started with Sourdough   153

How to Store Your Fresh Bread So That
It Lasts Longer   154

Make-Ahead Tips for Fitting Homemade Bread
into Your Busy Schedule   154

Thank Yous & Acknowledgments   159

About the Author   161

Index   162

INTRODUCTION

Just imagine—you open your front door and smell something . . . *amazing*. It's warm. It's a little buttery. You can't help but pause and breathe in more deeply.

What *is* that?

It's *home*.

Is this just a dream? Real life is crazy busy. Who comes home to something as special as homemade bread anymore? Long gone are the days when fresh bread was a standard part of family life. Now, we would be lucky to feature something even somewhat fresh from the local bakery in most meals we eat.

We've lost touch with what it means to "break bread" with our loved ones at the end of a long day. We've forgotten the comfort of passing the bread basket and sharing our stories. In our rush to do all the things in half the time, words like "homemade" and "from scratch" can sound utterly unattainable.

You and your loved ones deserve to experience that warm and heavenly smell right at home. When you pop a loaf of hot bread out of your bread machine, you aren't just serving up a practical side dish. You're showing your favorite people just how much you enjoy spending time with them around the table. You're inviting them to slow down, even if it's just long enough to butter up a slice of warm bread.

This unbelievable magic is merely a press of a button away. Homemade, 100 percent from scratch, completely warm and fresh bread is all yours with just a few minutes of adding ingredients to your bread pan and pressing "Start." No unique or advanced baking skills are required.

Let's just start and see what happens!

Flip the page and jump right in with The Quick Start Guide (page 10). It has everything you need to get a loaf baking in the next ten minutes. You probably have all the ingredients for the Milk & Honey Bread on page 17 in your pantry right now, but pick the recipe that calls to you. There's no perfect place to start.

Once you've ripped off that Band-Aid, you'll have questions. Be sure to check out the Common Questions from Newbie Bread Bakers and the other troubleshooting sections in Chapter 6 (page 144) for any extra help you might need.

Whether your old bread machine is simply collecting dust on the shelf or that new machine is staring you down from the box in the corner, my greatest hope is that the recipes in the following pages will inspire you to get it out, put it on the counter and make fresh bread a regular part of your weekly routine.

THE QUICK START GUIDE

There are two kinds of people in this world:

1. Those who read the manual cover to cover before starting.
2. The rest of us.

Why are manuals *so boring*? If you've ever thought, "This gizmo has one button on the front—how hard can it possibly be to use?" before turning it on and tossing the manual, this section is for you.

While I do have a chapter devoted to details and tips for the manual-lovers out there—check out Chapter 6 on page 144—the next couple pages are for the "I want bread for dinner tonight" people and will give you all the information you need to get your first bread baking in the next 10 minutes.

Step 1: Use the right yeast.

Every single recipe in this book uses the same exact yeast—instant yeast:

*   I recommend Saf-instant yeast or Fleischmann's instant yeast.

*   It **does not** need to be labeled "bread machine yeast," but if that's what you have, it will work just fine.

*   For the best value, buy a full package or jar, not the individual packets.

*   If you have some yeast on hand, make sure it was opened for the first time within the last three to six months or it may not work. Once opened, store your yeast in an airtight container in the fridge or freezer. You don't need to thaw or warm it before using it in a recipe.

Step 2: Use the right ingredients.

Butter: I used salted butter for every recipe throughout the book. If you prefer unsalted butter, you may want to add an extra pinch of salt to the recipe.

Milk: We always have 2% milk on hand in our fridge, so that's what I used in all of the recipes. You can also use 1% or whole milk, but skim milk will not have enough fat for the breads to work reliably.

Salt: Unless otherwise noted, kosher salt is my baking standby. It has the perfect texture and saltiness. Regular table salt will add too much saltiness and isn't a good substitute.

Step 3: For your first bread, choose the 1½-pound list of ingredients, NOT the 2-pound loaf.

Some 2-pound breads will be too large for some machines, even if the machine tells you it has that capacity. You're always safe with the 1½-pounders. I also recommend that you **test every recipe in the book with the 1½-pound loaf first so you can see how your machine handles it.** If the finished, baked loaf fills your pan more than three-fourths of the way, the 2-pound recipe will be too large for your machine.

Pick any bread from the book, except for the ones in the "Fun with Dough" chapter (page 111)—save those for after you've gotten to know your machine.

Step 4: Make sure your bread pan has the paddle attachment in place.

The paddle goes in first. Always.

If you forget, you'll have to fish around all the ingredients to get to the bottom of the pan to add it later—not fun. Ask my husband how we know this. He just might groan at the memory.

CUISINART COMPACT BREAD MAKER

The loaf bakes vertically and then is turned horizontally for slicing.

BREVILLE CUSTOM LOAF BREAD MAKER

The loaf bakes horizontally and is ready to be turned out of the pan for slicing.

Step 5: Add the ingredients to your bread machine baking pan in the *exact* order they are listed in the recipe.

Now is not the time to add things as you find them in the pantry. The order is crucial and is the difference between proper blending of the dough and having a bread that doesn't rise.

Take the pan out of the machine and put it on your counter. Unfortunate spills are easier to clean off the counter than from the inside of your machine.

Follow the recipe from top to bottom and watch for the mix-ins like chopped nuts and raisins, because they don't go in right away. Anything listed after "yeast" in the ingredients list is a mix-in, and the recipe will tell you when to add it. Be sure to check out page 151 for tips on weighing your ingredients to ensure a perfect loaf.

Once the pan is loaded up, add it back to your bread machine and close the lid.

Step 6: Select the correct settings on your bread machine.

Depending on your machine, there are just two or three settings you need to know:

Baking Program: First, select the corresponding baking program from the recipe (Basic/White, Whole Grain, Sweet, etc.).

Loaf Size: Select the 1½-pound loaf size. Remember to use this size with all new recipes; only choose the 2-pound size if you know your machine can accommodate it for that recipe.

Crust Darkness: Some machines let you choose between Light, Medium and Dark for the crust. Start with Light on all new recipes.

Step 6: Press START.

Your machine will mix, knead, rise and bake your loaf all by itself. You may have to add the mix-ins if you chose a recipe that includes them, but everything else should be done for you.

Step 7: Remove the bread from the machine within 5 to 10 minutes of the end of the bake cycle.

Don't rely on the "Keep Warm" setting that comes with most machines. Breads that stay in the bread pan too long can overbake, produce crusts that are too thick and dark or become wet and soggy from the steam.

If you can resist, wait 30 minutes to slice your bread. The knife will run through more easily and your bread will hold its shape far better.

If the heavenly aroma is just too enticing, you're in good company. Our family has enjoyed many mildly misshapen loaves that fell victim to our bread knives too soon. It's hard to beat that first warm slice when the butter melts the moment it touches the bread.

If you find you have questions that go a little deeper or you need to troubleshoot a recipe that didn't turn out as you hoped, be sure to check out Chapter 6 on page 144, which is filled with useful tidbits that will help you make perfect breads every time!

CHAPTER 1

CLASSIC BAKERY ESSENTIALS

Looking for your family's new favorite daily bread?

These loaves are the classic, all-purpose breads you'll turn to over and over again when you need the perfect breakfast toast, versatile sandwich builder or popular dinner dunker.

If you want just a touch of sweetness, be sure to test out the Milk & Honey (page 17), Brown Sugar Oatmeal (page 18) or Cinnamon Raisin (page 22) breads. With three totally different textures, you're sure to find your perfect match.

Need something a little heartier? Customize your perfect Caraway Rye Bread (page 26) or whip up a Steakhouse Brown Bread (page 29). You'll also discover just how easy it is to save an enormous amount of time by making homemade sourdoughs with your machine.

MILK & HONEY BREAD

BREAD MACHINE SETTING: BASIC/WHITE PROGRAM

Delicately sweet with a lightly textured crumb, this classic white bread is an essential everyday loaf. You can enhance the flavor by swapping in different varietals of honey. Our family's favorite is a sweet and slightly tangy orange blossom honey.

1½-POUND LOAF	2-POUND LOAF
½ cup (120 g) water	⅔ cup (160 g) water
½ cup (120 g) milk	⅔ cup (160 g) milk
1½ tbsp (12 g) canola oil	2 tbsp (16 g) canola oil
2 tbsp (42 g) honey	3 tbsp (63 g) honey
3 cups (411 g) bread flour	4 cups (548 g) bread flour
1 tsp (6 g) kosher salt	1½ tsp (9 g) kosher salt
1¾ tsp (5.5 g) yeast	2¼ tsp (7 g) yeast

Add the ingredients to your bread machine's baking pan in the order they are listed, starting with the water and ending with the yeast.

Choose the Basic/White program setting based on your machine's options. Select the coordinating setting for your loaf size on your machine and press Start.

When the loaf is done, remove it from the baking pan and transfer it to a wire rack to cool for at least 30 minutes before slicing.

SERVING SUGGESTIONS

Toast slices and spread with butter, then top with a sprinkle of cinnamon sugar for breakfast.

Spread with cream cheese and thinly sliced cucumbers and cut into finger sandwiches.

This bread is excellent for egg or chicken salad sandwiches.

BROWN SUGAR OATMEAL BREAD

BREAD MACHINE SETTING: WHOLE GRAIN OR BASIC/WHITE PROGRAM

Warm, comforting, chewy oatmeal bread is the loaf you didn't know you needed.
The hearty texture of this bread stands up to whatever thick and creamy fillings you
want to add to your sandwich.

1½-POUND LOAF	2-POUND LOAF
⅔ cup (160 g) milk	¾ cup (180 g) milk
⅓ cup (80 g) water	½ cup (120 g) water
1 tbsp (14 g) butter, softened and cut into pieces	2 tbsp (28 g) butter, softened and cut into pieces
2½ cups (342 g) bread flour	3⅓ cups (452 g) bread flour
1 cup (90 g) quick cooking rolled oats (see Note)	1⅓ cups (107 g) quick cooking rolled oats (see Note)
3 tbsp (42 g) packed brown sugar	¼ cup (55 g) packed brown sugar
¾ tsp (4.5 g) kosher salt	1 tsp (6 g) kosher salt
1 tsp (3 g) yeast	1¼ tsp (3.7 g) yeast

Add the ingredients to your bread machine's baking pan in the order they are listed, starting with the milk and ending with the yeast.

Choose the Whole Grain or Basic/White program setting based on your machine's options. Select the coordinating setting for your loaf size on your machine and press Start.

When the loaf is done, remove it from the bread pan and transfer it to a wire rack to cool for at least 30 minutes before slicing.

NOTE: Quick cooking rolled oats will absorb more easily into the bread dough during baking. If you do not have them on hand, you can use regular rolled oats, but the texture of the bread will be a little heartier.

SERVING SUGGESTIONS

Make a hearty breakfast sandwich with fried eggs and a sweet maple breakfast sausage patty.

Toast a slice, spread with peanut butter and top it with fresh sliced bananas.

This bread gives a lovely extra chew to a marshmallow fluffernutter sandwich.

HONEY WHOLE WHEAT BREAD

BREAD MACHINE SETTING: WHOLE GRAIN OR BASIC/WHITE PROGRAM

Ease your kids into eating more whole grains with this tender, honey-sweetened loaf. Mixing whole wheat with bread flour keeps the crumb texture light while giving the bread a lovely nutty flavor that won't overwhelm any picky eaters.

1½-POUND LOAF	2-POUND LOAF
⅓ cup (80 g) water	½ cup (120 g) water
½ cup (120 g) milk	⅔ cup (160 g) milk
¼ cup (84 g) honey	⅓ cup (112 g) honey
1 large egg	1 large egg
1 tbsp (14 g) butter, softened and cut into pieces	1½ tbsp (21 g) butter, softened and cut into pieces
2 cups (274 g) bread flour	2⅔ cups (365 g) bread flour
1 cup (137 g) whole wheat flour	1⅓ cups (183 g) whole wheat flour
2 tsp (12 g) kosher salt	2½ tsp (15 g) kosher salt
2¼ tsp (7 g) yeast	1 tbsp (9 g) yeast

Add the ingredients to your bread machine's baking pan in the order they are listed, starting with the water and ending with the yeast.

Choose the Whole Grain or Basic/White program setting based on your machine's options. Select the coordinating setting for your loaf size on your machine and press Start.

When the loaf is done, remove it from the bread pan and transfer it to a wire rack to cool for at least 30 minutes before slicing.

SERVING SUGGESTIONS

Griddle a slice with a touch of olive oil for your favorite avocado toast.

Try a grilled Elvis sandwich by spreading creamy peanut butter and topping with some crispy bacon and a smashed banana.

Layer thinly cut fresh veggies with a slathering of herbed cream cheese for a Mediterranean sandwich.

CINNAMON RAISIN BREAD

BREAD MACHINE SETTING: WHOLE GRAIN OR BASIC/WHITE PROGRAM

A comforting childhood staple—raisin toast spread with melty butter—is even better when you start with a fresh, warm loaf and slice the pieces just as thickly as you want! You can control just how many raisins you want in your bread, but we think this is the perfect amount!

1½-POUND LOAF
1 cup (240 g) water
3 tbsp (63 g) honey
2 tbsp (28 g) butter, softened and cut into pieces
2 cups (274 g) bread flour
1 cup (137 g) whole wheat flour
¾ tsp (4.5 g) kosher salt
1 tsp (2.6 g) ground cinnamon
1 tsp (3 g) yeast

MIX-INS
½ cup (84 g) raisins, plumped (see directions)

2-POUND LOAF
1⅓ cups (320 g) water
¼ cup (84 g) honey
3 tbsp (42 g) butter, softened and cut into pieces
2¾ cups (376 g) bread flour
1¼ cups (171 g) whole wheat flour
1 tsp (6 g) kosher salt
1½ tsp (4 g) ground cinnamon
1¼ tsp (3.7 g) yeast

MIX-INS
¾ cup (124 g) raisins, plumped (see directions)

To plump your raisins before baking, microwave 1 cup (240 g) of water for 3 minutes and soak the raisins in the hot water for 10 minutes. Alternatively, you could bring the water to boil in a saucepan on your stovetop. Remove the pan from the heat and soak the raisins for 10 minutes. Spread the raisins out on a paper towel to drain. Reserve the raisins for the mix-in phase of kneading.

Add the ingredients to your bread machine's baking pan in the order listed, from water to yeast. Set the raisins next to your machine so they are ready to be added at the mix-in phase.

Choose the Whole Grain or Basic/White program setting based on your machine's options. Select the coordinating setting for your loaf size on your machine and press Start.

When your machine beeps, add the raisins to the bread pan. This happens between the second and third knead cycle.

When the loaf is done, remove it from the baking pan and transfer it to a wire rack to cool for at least 30 minutes before slicing.

SERVING SUGGESTIONS

Put a delicious twist on French toast and garnish with a sprinkle of powdered sugar and an extra dash of cinnamon.

Sandwich two pieces with a cream cheese filling and cut into strips for a simple lunch.

Cube your loaf for a classic raisin bread pudding.

ITALIAN BREAD

BREAD MACHINE SETTING: BASIC/WHITE PROGRAM

This is the bread that started our obsession with bread machines! Light and simple, it makes an amazing dunker for soups and deliciously chewy toast. You'll find dozens of dinners where it becomes the perfect companion.

1½-POUND LOAF
¾ cup (180 g) milk
3 tbsp (45 g) water
1 large egg
1 tbsp (14 g) butter, softened and cut into pieces
3 cups (411 g) bread flour
1 tsp (4 g) sugar
½ tsp (3 g) kosher salt
1¼ tsp (3.7 g) yeast

2-POUND LOAF
1 cup (240 g) milk
¼ cup (60 g) water
1 large egg
1½ tbsp (21 g) butter, softened and cut into pieces
4 cups (548 g) bread flour
1¼ tsp (5 g) sugar
¾ tsp (4.5 g) kosher salt
1½ tsp (4.5 g) yeast

Add the ingredients to your bread machine's baking pan in the order listed, from milk to yeast.

Choose the Basic/White program setting based on your machine's options. Select the coordinating setting for your loaf size on your machine and press Start.

When the loaf is done, remove it from the bread pan and transfer it to a wire rack to cool for at least 30 minutes before slicing.

SERVING SUGGESTIONS

Serve fresh, warm slices of this versatile bread with any soup or stew for dunking.

Toast it and spread with butter, a sprinkle of garlic salt and grated Parmesan cheese for a single serving of garlic bread.

Cut slices into four triangles, brush with olive oil and toast a large batch under the broiler. Serve alongside a bowl of tomato bruschetta for topping.

CARAWAY RYE BREAD

BREAD MACHINE SETTING: WHOLE GRAIN OR BASIC/WHITE PROGRAM

No need to go to the deli or diner for a decent rye bread. This homemade version lets you control just how many caraway seeds are involved. Try sprinkling coarse sea salt over the top of the loaf after the last rise for a pretty, salted rye.

1½-POUND LOAF
1 cup (240 g) water
2 tbsp (28 g) butter, softened and cut into pieces
2 cups (274 g) bread flour
1 cup (137 g) rye flour
2 tbsp (28 g) packed brown sugar
2 tsp (4 g) caraway seed
¾ tsp (4.5 g) kosher salt
1 tsp (3 g) yeast

2-POUND LOAF
1⅓ cups (320 g) water
3 tbsp (42 g) butter, softened and cut into pieces
2⅔ cups (365 g) bread flour
1⅓ cups (183 g) rye flour
3 tbsp (42 g) packed brown sugar
1 tbsp (6.7 g) caraway seed
1 tsp (6 g) kosher salt
1¼ tsp (3.7 g) yeast

Add the ingredients to your bread machine's baking pan in the order listed, from water to yeast.

Choose the Whole Grain program setting if your machine offers it. Otherwise, the Basic/White program setting will work just as well. Select the coordinating setting for your loaf size on your machine and press Start.

When the loaf is done, remove it from the bread pan and transfer it to a wire rack to cool for at least 30 minutes before slicing.

SERVING SUGGESTIONS

Griddle up corned beef or sliced turkey, Swiss cheese, sauerkraut and Thousand Island dressing for a classic Reuben sandwich.

Slather a slice with cream cheese and top with smoked salmon, thinly sliced cucumber and fresh chives.

This bread is delicious alongside rich or spicy tomato-based soups or as a side for beef goulash instead of pasta.

STEAKHOUSE BROWN BREAD

BREAD MACHINE SETTING: BASIC/WHITE PROGRAM

Deep brown and utterly delicious with whipped honey butter, this loaf is so good it's no wonder why your local steak joint serves it up before dinner. No need to be fussy; serve it on a wooden cutting board with a bread knife and let everyone at the table cut chunks or wedges of bread to share.

1½-POUND LOAF	2-POUND LOAF
1 cup (240 g) water	1¼ cups (300 g) water
3 tbsp (63 g) molasses	¼ cup (84 g) molasses
2 tbsp (42 g) honey	3 tbsp (63 g) honey
1½ tbsp (12 g) cooking oil	2 tbsp (16 g) cooking oil
2 cups (274 g) bread flour	2⅔ cups (365 g) bread flour
1 cup (137 g) whole wheat flour	1⅓ cups (183 g) whole wheat flour
1 tsp (2 g) unsweetened cocoa powder	1¼ tsp (2.5 g) unsweetened cocoa powder
1 tsp (6 g) kosher salt	1¼ tsp (7.5 g) kosher salt
2 tsp (6 g) yeast	2¼ tsp (7 g) yeast

Add the ingredients to your bread machine's baking pan in the order listed, from water to yeast.

Choose the Basic/White program setting based on your machine's options. Select the coordinating setting for your loaf size on your machine and press Start.

When the loaf is done, remove it from the bread pan and transfer it to a wire rack to cool for at least 30 minutes before slicing.

SERVING SUGGESTIONS

Slice a freshly warm loaf and serve with a beef stew or hamburger soup.

Griddle a sandwich layered with slices of brie, thinly cut green apples and a drizzle of honey.

Prepare the ingredients in the bread pan as directed but select the Dough program. Follow the instructions for the Buttery Dinner Rolls (page 118) for finishing in the oven.

EVERYTHING BAGEL BREAD

BREAD MACHINE SETTING: BASIC/WHITE PROGRAM

This easy, savory bubble bread has layers of melted butter and everything bagel seasoning sprinkled throughout. It bakes into a solid, sliceable loaf for serving once completely cooled.

1½-POUND LOAF
¾ cup (180 g) milk
3 tbsp (42 g) butter, softened and cut into pieces
1 large egg
3 cups (411 g) all-purpose flour
1 tbsp (12.5 g) sugar
1 tsp (6 g) kosher salt
2 tsp (6 g) yeast

2-POUND LOAF
1 cup (240 g) milk
¼ cup (56 g) butter, softened and cut into pieces
1 large egg
4 cups (548 g) all-purpose flour
1½ tbsp (18.8 g) sugar
1½ tsp (9 g) kosher salt
2½ tsp (7.5 g) yeast

EVERYTHING BAGEL TOPPING
1–2 tbsp (14–28 g) everything bagel seasoning
3 tbsp (42 g) butter, melted

Add the ingredients to your bread machine's baking pan in the order listed, from milk to yeast.

Choose the Basic/White program setting based on your machine's options. Select the coordinating setting for your loaf size on your machine and press Start.

After the last knead cycle and before the third rise, transfer the dough to a baking mat. Remove the paddle and divide the dough into 14 to 16 golf ball–sized pieces. Quickly form them into ball shapes.

Lightly nestle the dough balls back into the machine and be sure to avoid packing them too tightly. Depending on your pan shape, they will likely be in more than one layer. Sprinkle the seasoning and drizzle the melted butter over each layer as you add the dough to the pan. Drizzle the last of the butter and give a final sprinkle of the seasoning over the top of the dough. Return the pan to the machine and let it finish the last rise and bake cycle.

When the loaf is done, let the bread cool in the pan for 5 to 10 minutes before removing it. Transfer the bread to a wire rack to cool for at least 30 minutes before slicing.

NOTE: To make your own everything bagel seasoning, mix together 1 tablespoon (14 g) of poppy seeds, 1 tablespoon (14 g) of sesame seeds, 1 teaspoon (7 g) of dried minced onion, 1 teaspoon (3 g) of dried garlic flakes and 2 teaspoons (6 g) of sea salt.

SERVING SUGGESTIONS

Serve instead of bagels at brunch with homemade omelets or scrambled eggs.

The savory bread pairs well with mild chicken-based or light veggie and tomato-based soups; it also works well as a replacement for regular garlic bread.

SPEEDY SOURDOUGH LOAF

BREAD MACHINE SETTING: CRUSTY BREAD OR DOUGH PROGRAM + CUSTOM BAKE FOR 60 MINUTES

You can save days' worth of your time by making sourdough bread in your bread machine. Skip right over the long overnight rises and wait times and have a tangy, chewy loaf out of your machine in just hours. Be sure to check out page 153 for all the tips you need for using sourdough starter.

1½-POUND LOAF	2-POUND LOAF
3 tbsp (45 g) water, cool	½ cup (120 g) water, cool
2 cups (400 g) sourdough starter, room temperature	2½ cups (500 g) sourdough starter, room temperature
2½ cups (342 g) bread flour	3 cups (411 g) bread flour
1 tsp (4 g) sugar	1½ tsp (6 g) sugar
1½ tsp (9 g) kosher salt	2 tsp (12 g) kosher salt
2 tsp (6 g) yeast	2½ tsp (7.5 g) yeast

Add the ingredients to your bread machine's baking pan in the order they are listed, starting with the water and ending with the yeast.

If your machine offers it, choose the Crusty Bread setting for the perfect crust. Select the coordinating setting for your loaf size on your machine and press Start.

If your machine doesn't offer the Crusty Bread program, you'll need to use the regular Dough program (avoid Artisan Dough) to rise the dough in the machine. Then either set a custom 60 minute bake time after the dough has finished rising or transfer your bread to a loaf pan and bake it in your regular oven. See the full instructions for baking bread in your oven on page 112. In a pinch, the White program would also work but will not give as crispy of a crust.

When the loaf is done, remove it from the bread pan and transfer it to a wire rack to cool for at least 30 minutes before slicing. If the crust is a little too hearty for your preference, it will soften up overnight in a bread bag or bread box on your counter.

SERVING SUGGESTIONS

Toast and spread with Nutella and fresh strawberries.

Griddle sandwiches with layers of thinly sliced steak, white cheddar and caramelized onions.

Layer thinly sliced chicken, pesto, fresh tomatoes and slices of mozzarella and griddle a panini with a touch of olive oil.

SOURDOUGH PESTO SWIRL

BREAD MACHINE SETTING: BASIC/WHITE PROGRAM

This chewy, Italian herb sourdough bakes up easily with prepared pesto from the grocery store. No extra time is needed chopping fresh basil or grating that good salty Parmesan— you'll get all that extra flavor with just a simple dollop. Make sure to take a look at page 153 for my tips about using sourdough starter.

1½-POUND LOAF	2-POUND LOAF
1 cup (200 g) sourdough starter, room temperature	1⅓ cups (266 g) sourdough starter, room temperature
½ cup (120 g) milk	½ cup (120 g) milk
2 tbsp (16 g) olive oil	3 tbsp (24 g) olive oil
3 tbsp (45 g) pesto	¼ cup (60 g) pesto
3 cups (411 g) bread flour	4 cups (548 g) bread flour
1 tbsp (12.5 g) sugar	1½ tbsp (18.8 g) sugar
½ tsp (3 g) garlic salt	¾ tsp (4.5 g) garlic salt
2 tsp (5 g) Italian herb blend	2½ tsp (6.3 g) Italian herb blend
½ tsp (3 g) kosher salt	¾ tsp (4.5 g) kosher salt
1½ tsp (4.5 g) yeast	1¾ tsp (5.5 g) yeast

Add the ingredients to your bread machine's baking pan in the order they are listed, starting with the sourdough starter and ending with the yeast.

Choose the Basic/White program setting based on your machine's options. Select the coordinating setting for your loaf size on your machine and press Start.

When the loaf is done, remove it from the bread pan and transfer it to a wire rack to cool for at least 30 minutes before slicing.

SERVING SUGGESTIONS

Build a Caprese sandwich with some fresh mozzarella, basil and sliced tomatoes. Drizzle with a touch of balsamic vinegar.

Griddle a veggie sandwich with breaded eggplant cutlets, fresh tomatoes and slices of provolone.

Serve this bread instead of regular Italian bread as a side dish for fresh chicken Caesar salad or pasta night.

CHAPTER 2

SOUP & SANDWICH PARTNERS

Fresh bread goes with soup and sandwiches like macaroni goes with cheese. The easiest way to spice up a monotonous dinner rut is to pair up a brand-new bread with one of your family's favorite recipes. Does everyone love your veggie soup? Try serving it with warm slices of Savory Swiss & Onion Bread (page 43) or Loaded Baked Potato Bread (page 51). Is your BBQ chicken a hit? Shred it and make sandwiches out of the Jalapeño Popper Cornbread (page 56) or Savory Sweet Potato Bread (page 44). Is slow-cooked beef stew your go-to busy night meal? Next time, add a Honeyed Blue Cheese (page 52) or Rosemary Herb (page 39) bread for a stellar side dish.

In this chapter, you'll find oodles of inspiration for easy family meals using some of our favorite savory breads.

ROSEMARY HERB BREAD

BREAD MACHINE SETTING: BASIC/WHITE PROGRAM

Whether paired with a soup or sandwich, this lightly flavored bread is one of the most versatile recipes for your menu. You'll be ready to bake it in a pinch using pantry-staple dried herbs, but it is a great recipe for using up the last of any fresh herbs from your fridge.

1½-POUND LOAF

1 cup + 2 tbsp (270 g) water

1½ tbsp (12 g) olive oil

3¼ cups (445 g) bread flour

1 tbsp (12.5 g) sugar

1½ tsp (9 g) kosher salt

1 tsp (1 g) dried rosemary or 1 tbsp (2 g) fresh rosemary, minced

½ tsp (1 g) dried oregano or ½ tbsp (2 g) fresh oregano

½ tsp (1 g) dried basil or ½ tbsp (2 g) fresh basil

½ tsp (1 g) fresh cracked pepper

2 tsp (6 g) yeast

2-POUND LOAF

1½ cups (360 g) water

2 tbsp (16 g) olive oil

4 cups (548 g) bread flour

1½ tbsp (18.8 g) sugar

2 tsp (12 g) kosher salt

1½ tsp (2 g) dried rosemary or 1½ tbsp (3 g) fresh rosemary, minced

1 tsp (2 g) dried oregano or 1 tbsp (3 g) fresh oregano

1 tsp (2 g) dried basil or 1 tbsp (3 g) fresh basil

1 tsp (2 g) fresh cracked pepper

2¼ tsp (7 g) yeast

Add the ingredients to your bread machine's baking pan in the order they are listed, starting with the water and ending with the yeast.

Select the Basic/White program depending on your machine's options. Then set the coordinating settings for your loaf size and press Start.

When the loaf is done, remove it from the bread pan and transfer it to a wire rack to cool for at least 30 minutes before slicing.

SERVING SUGGESTIONS

Slice and serve as a side dish for pot roast, beef stew or roast chicken.

Sandwich slices pair especially well with deli roast beef, horseradish sauce and fresh tomatoes.

Dunk this savory bread in a bowl of minestrone, Italian wedding, tortellini & spinach or chicken noodle soup.

FARMERS' MARKET VEGGIE PATCH BREAD

BREAD MACHINE SETTING: BASIC/WHITE PROGRAM

Colorful sprinkles of garden-fresh veggies bring a party of flavors to this healthy bread. The shredded vegetables practically melt into the dough, making this an excellent choice for even the pickiest of eaters.

1½-POUND LOAF	2-POUND LOAF
¾ cup (180 g) water	1 cup (240 g) water
½ cup (55 g) shredded carrots	⅔ cup (73 g) shredded carrots
⅓ cup (72 g) shredded zucchini	½ cup (108 g) shredded zucchini
2 green onions, green and white parts, minced	3 green onions, green and white parts, minced
¼ cup (44 g) finely chopped red bell pepper	⅓ cup (59 g) finely chopped red bell pepper
1 tbsp (14 g) butter, softened and cut into pieces	1½ tbsp (21 g) butter, softened and cut into pieces
3 cups (411 g) bread flour	4 cups (548 g) bread flour
1 tsp (4 g) sugar	1½ tsp (6 g) sugar
¾ tsp (4.5 g) kosher salt	1 tsp (6 g) kosher salt
½ tsp (1 g) dried thyme or ½ tbsp (1 g) fresh thyme	¾ tsp (2 g) dried thyme or 1 tbsp (3 g) fresh thyme
1 tsp (3 g) yeast	1¼ tsp (3.7 g) yeast

Add the ingredients to your bread machine's baking pan in the order they are listed, from water to yeast. Do not squeeze the liquid out of the zucchini because it will help add moisture to the dough.

Select the Basic/White program according to your machine's options. Then select the coordinating settings for your loaf size and press Start.

Keep an eye on the dough as it mixes. The vegetables will begin to release extra liquid during the kneading process. You may need to add a tablespoon or two (8.5 to 17 g) of bread flour if the dough begins to stick too much to the sides of the pan.

When the loaf is done, remove it from the bread pan and transfer it to a wire rack to cool for at least 30 minutes before slicing.

SERVING SUGGESTIONS

This bread is perfect for the ultimate turkey sandwich—just add baby spinach, fresh tomatoes and your favorite cheese.

Pair slices with a big bowl of roasted red pepper soup or your favorite creamy vegetable soup.

Make uniquely delicious croutons for a garden salad by tossing cubed chunks of day-old bread with a drizzle of olive oil and baking in an even layer at 375°F (190°C) for approximately 15 minutes.

SAVORY SWISS & ONION BREAD

BREAD MACHINE SETTING: BASIC/WHITE PROGRAM

Freshly chopped yellow onion and shredded Swiss cheese practically melt into the bread dough for this savory loaf, giving it an amazingly smooth texture. Each slice bursts with flavor but you'll find the onion doesn't overwhelm your sandwich.

1½-POUND LOAF	2-POUND LOAF
¼ cup (40 g) finely chopped yellow onion	⅓ cup (53 g) finely chopped yellow onion
½ cup (120 g) milk	⅔ cup (160 g) milk
¼ cup (60 g) water	⅓ cup (80 g) water
1 tbsp (14 g) butter, softened and cut into pieces	1½ tbsp (21 g) butter, softened and cut into pieces
1 large egg	1 large egg
1 cup (80 g) shredded Swiss cheese	1⅓ cups (105 g) shredded Swiss cheese
2¼ cups (308 g) bread flour	2¾ cups (376 g) bread flour
¾ cup (103 g) whole wheat flour	1¼ cups (171 g) whole wheat flour
¾ tsp (1.8 g) caraway seed	1 tsp (3 g) caraway seed
½ tsp (3 g) kosher salt	¾ tsp (4.5 g) kosher salt
1 tsp (3 g) yeast	1¼ tsp (3.7 g) yeast

Add the ingredients to your bread machine's baking pan in the order they are listed, starting with the chopped onion and ending with the yeast. The Swiss cheese will melt right into the dough and should be added with the liquids.

Select the Basic/White program according to the options on your machine. Then select the coordinating settings for your loaf size and press Start.

When the loaf is done, remove it from the bread pan and transfer it to a wire rack to cool for at least 30 minutes before slicing.

SERVING SUGGESTIONS

Slice and dunk in beef broth–based soups like French onion or vegetable beef.

Layer sliced ham, mustard and Gruyère for grown-up grilled cheese sandwiches.

Cube a one- or two-day old loaf and use in a savory egg strata with baby spinach.

SAVORY SWEET POTATO BREAD

BREAD MACHINE SETTING: BASIC/WHITE PROGRAM

For all the flavor but none of the effort, a simple jar of sweet potato baby food is the perfect pantry secret to this delicious savory loaf. Fresh green onions brighten up each slice and give the perfect kick to your leftover Thanksgiving turkey sandwich.

1½-POUND LOAF	2-POUND LOAF
1 (6-oz [170-g]) jar sweet potato baby food or 6 oz (170 g) canned sweet potato puree	1 (6-oz [170-g]) jar sweet potato baby food or 6 oz (170 g) canned sweet potato puree
⅓ cup (80 g) water	½ cup (120 g) water
1 tbsp (14 g) butter, softened and cut into pieces	1½ tbsp (21 g) butter, softened and cut into pieces
⅓ cup (32 g) sliced green onions	½ cup (48 g) sliced green onions
3 cups (411 g) bread flour	4 cups (548 g) bread flour
1 tsp (4 g) sugar	1¼ tsp (5 g) sugar
1 tsp (1 g) dried thyme or 1 tbsp (2 g) fresh thyme	1¼ tsp (1 g) dried thyme or 1 tbsp (2 g) fresh thyme
¾ tsp (4.5 g) kosher salt	1 tsp (6 g) kosher salt
1 tsp (3 g) yeast	1¼ tsp (3.7 g) yeast

Add the ingredients to your bread machine's baking pan in the order they are listed, starting with the sweet potato puree and ending with the yeast.

Select the Basic/White program depending on your machine's options. Then set the coordinating loaf size and press Start.

When the loaf is done, remove it from the bread pan and transfer it to a wire rack to cool for at least 30 minutes before slicing.

SERVING SUGGESTIONS

Make a classic Thanksgiving sandwich with leftover turkey and cranberry sauce.

Slice and dunk hearty slices in mulligatawny or spicy coconut chicken soups.

Serve as a savory side dish with some BBQ chicken.

CUCUMBER DILL TZATZIKI BREAD

BREAD MACHINE SETTING: BASIC/WHITE PROGRAM

With all the flavors of your favorite Greek restaurant rolled into each loaf, this bread is the perfect partner for a light salad or Mediterranean meal. The sour cream and shredded cucumber help create an especially light and tender bread.

1½-POUND LOAF

¾ cup (100 g) peeled and shredded cucumber (English or seedless)
½ cup (120 g) water
⅓ cup (82 g) sour cream
3¼ cups (445 g) bread flour
2 tsp (8 g) sugar
¾ tsp (4.5 g) kosher salt
½ tsp (0.3 g) dried dill or ½ tbsp (1.6 g) fresh dill
1 tsp (3 g) yeast

2-POUND LOAF

1 cup (133 g) peeled and shredded cucumber (English or seedless)
⅔ cup (160 g) water
½ cup (123 g) sour cream
4½ cups (617 g) bread flour
1 tbsp (12.5 g) sugar
1 tsp (6 g) kosher salt
¾ tsp (0.5 g) dried dill or ½ tbsp (2 g) fresh dill
1¼ tsp (3.7 g) yeast

Add the ingredients to your bread machine's baking pan in the order they are listed, starting with the shredded cucumber and ending with the yeast. Do not squeeze the juices out of the cucumber like you would for traditional tzatziki because you need the liquid from the veggies to keep the dough ratio intact.

Select the Basic/White program depending on your machine. Then, select the coordinating setting for your loaf size on your machine and press Start.

When the loaf is done, remove it from the bread pan and transfer it to a wire rack to cool for at least 30 minutes before slicing.

SERVING SUGGESTIONS

Cut slices into squares and toast under the broiler to make some simple crostini for a summery charcuterie board or to serve alongside roasted pepper bruschetta.

Toast a few slices to pair with a bright lemon chicken or Greek avgolemono soup.

Enjoy as a side dish with some roasted salmon or spiced grilled shrimp.

SUN-DRIED TOMATO PARMESAN BREAD

BREAD MACHINE SETTING: BASIC/WHITE PROGRAM

It's time to level-up your regular turkey sandwich with this flavor-packed, tomato-infused bread. A bit of whole wheat gives each slice an excellent chew while the tomato sauce gives the loaf a gorgeous color.

1½-POUND LOAF	2-POUND LOAF
⅔ cup (160 g) water	¾ cup (180 g) water
3 tbsp (20 g) sun-dried tomatoes in oil, cut finely	¼ cup (27 g) sun-dried tomatoes in oil, cut finely
½ cup (112 g) canned tomato sauce	¾ cup (169 g) canned tomato sauce
1 tbsp (14 g) butter, softened and cut into pieces	1½ tbsp (21 g) butter, softened and cut into pieces
1 cup (80 g) shredded Parmesan	1⅓ cups (100 g) shredded Parmesan
2 cups (274 g) bread flour	2⅔ cups (365 g) bread flour
1 cup (137 g) whole wheat flour	1⅓ cups (183 g) whole wheat flour
1 tbsp (14 g) packed brown sugar	2 tbsp (28 g) packed brown sugar
1 tsp (1 g) Italian herb blend	1½ tsp (4 g) Italian herb blend
½ tsp (3 g) kosher salt	¾ tsp (4.5 g) kosher salt
1 tsp (3 g) yeast	1¼ tsp (3.7 g) yeast

Add the ingredients to your bread machine's baking pan in the order they are listed, starting with the water and ending with the yeast. The shredded Parmesan will melt right into the dough and should be added with the liquids.

Select the Basic/White program depending on your machine's options. Then select the coordinating setting for your loaf size on your machine and press Start.

When the loaf is done, remove it from the bread pan and transfer it to a wire rack to cool for at least 30 minutes before slicing.

SERVING SUGGESTIONS

Assemble an incredible Italian grinder with layers of Genoa salami, capicola, pepperoni and mozzarella cheese.

Griddle up leftover roasted peppers and onions with provolone cheese for a flavorful grilled cheese and pair with an Italian wedding soup.

Toast a couple of slices and make an open-faced meatball sandwich. Sprinkle mozzarella over the top and melt it under the broiler.

LOADED BAKED POTATO BREAD

BREAD MACHINE SETTING: BASIC/WHITE PROGRAM

Get all the flavors of the classic sports bar appetizer in every slice of this hearty loaf. Leftover mashed potatoes from your holiday dinner or a tub of prepared potatoes from the store keep the recipe extra easy.

1½-POUND LOAF
¾ cup (188 g) prepared mashed potatoes, warmed
⅓ cup (80 g) milk
½ cup (40 g) shredded sharp cheddar cheese
1 tbsp (14 g) butter, softened and cut into pieces
3 cups (411 g) bread flour
1 tbsp (12.5 g) sugar
¼ tsp (0.7 g) onion powder
¾ tsp (4.5 g) kosher salt
¼ tsp (0.7 g) ground pepper
3 tbsp (9 g) fresh chives, minced
1 tsp (3 g) yeast

MIX-INS
3 strips of bacon, cooked and crumbled

2-POUND LOAF
1 cup (250 g) prepared mashed potatoes, warmed
⅔ cup (160 g) milk
⅔ cup (53 g) shredded sharp cheddar cheese
2 tbsp (28 g) butter, softened and cut into pieces
4 cups (548 g) bread flour
1½ tbsp (18.8 g) sugar
½ tsp (2 g) onion powder
1 tsp (6 g) kosher salt
½ tsp (2 g) ground pepper
¼ cup (12 g) fresh chives, minced
1¼ tsp (3.7 g) yeast

MIX-INS
4 strips of bacon, cooked and crumbled

Add the ingredients to your bread machine's baking pan in the order they are listed, starting with the mashed potatoes and ending with the yeast. The shredded cheddar will melt right into the dough and should be added with the liquids. Reserve the bacon for the mix-in phase.

Select the Basic/White program based on your machine's options. Then, select the coordinating setting for your loaf size on your machine and press Start.

Most machines will alert you with a beep when it is time to add the bacon crumbles. If yours does not, add them to the machine in the middle of the second knead cycle.

When the loaf is done, remove it from the bread pan and transfer it to a wire rack to cool for at least 30 minutes before slicing.

SERVING SUGGESTIONS

Enjoy alongside a BBQ chicken salad or dunk in a creamy beer cheese soup.

Grill extra thin hamburgers and make a tasty homemade patty melt sandwich.

Serve as a side dish for meatloaf or roasted pork tenderloin.

HONEYED BLUE CHEESE BREAD

BREAD MACHINE SETTING: BASIC/WHITE PROGRAM

The beauty of the bread machine is that you can customize the flavors to fit your family. You can adjust the amount of blue cheese in this recipe to have just a hint of flavor or to pack a powerful punch, as this recipe falls just about in the middle. Sweet honey and savory thyme help balance it out.

1½-POUND LOAF	2-POUND LOAF
½ cup (120 g) milk	⅔ cup (160 g) milk
¼ cup (60 g) water	⅓ cup (80 g) water
¼ cup (34 g) blue cheese crumbles	⅓ cup (45 g) blue cheese crumbles
1 tbsp (21 g) honey	1½ tbsp (31 g) honey
1 tbsp (14 g) butter, softened and cut into pieces	1½ tbsp (21 g) butter, softened and cut into pieces
3 cups (411 g) bread flour	4 cups (548 g) bread flour
1 tsp (1 g) dried thyme or 1 tbsp (2 g) fresh thyme	1½ tsp (1 g) dried thyme or 1 tbsp (2 g) fresh thyme
½ tsp (3 g) kosher salt	¾ tsp (4.5 g) kosher salt
1 tsp (3 g) yeast	1¼ tsp (3.7 g) yeast

Add the ingredients to your bread machine's baking pan in the order they are listed, starting with the milk and ending with the yeast. The blue cheese will melt right into the dough and should be added with the liquids.

Select the Basic/White program based on your machine's options. Then select the coordinating setting for your loaf size on your machine and press Start.

When the loaf is done, remove it from the bread pan and transfer it to a wire rack to cool for at least 30 minutes before slicing.

SERVING SUGGESTIONS

Slices of this bread pair well with sandwiches of sliced roast beef or a tart chicken salad made with dried cranberries.

Serve alongside a steak salad with fresh greens, chopped pistachios and a mustard vinaigrette.

Make a buffalo chicken sandwich with shredded chicken and a drizzle of ranch.

BEER FLIGHT BREAD

BREAD MACHINE SETTING: BASIC/WHITE PROGRAM

If you've curiously eyed up the enormous variety of flavored beers and ciders at your local store, this simple, slightly sweetened bread recipe is the perfect place to give them a whirl. Buy just a single bottle or can of something new and give it a test drive. Our favorite so far is Sam Adams Winter or Alpine Lager with a hint of cinnamon, ginger and orange peel.

1½-POUND LOAF	2-POUND LOAF
1 cup + 2 tbsp (9 oz [250 g]) beer	1½ cups (12 oz [354 g]) beer
2 tbsp (16 g) olive oil	3 tbsp (24 g) olive oil
3½ cups (480 g) bread flour	4½ cups (617 g) bread flour
¼ cup (50 g) sugar	⅓ cup (66 g) sugar
¾ tsp (4.5 g) salt	1 tsp (6 g) salt
1¾ tsp (5.5 g) yeast	2½ tsp (7.5 g) yeast

Open the beer and pour it into a measuring cup. Let it sit at room temperature for a few hours so that it goes flat. The carbonation in a fresh beer would negatively affect how the bread rises so be sure not to skip this step. If you're in a rush, pour the beer into a large bowl and stir it gently for several minutes to speed up the flattening process.

Add the ingredients to your bread machine's baking pan in the order they are listed, starting with the beer and ending with the yeast.

Select the Basic/White program based on your machine's options. Then select the coordinating setting for your loaf size on your machine and press Start.

When the loaf is done, remove it from the bread pan and transfer it to a wire rack to cool for at least 30 minutes before slicing.

SERVING SUGGESTIONS

Slice and cut this bread into squares, toast a large batch under the broiler and serve with a hot and creamy spinach dip.

Cube the loaf and use for dunking into a hot cheese fondue.

Serve hearty slices alongside a thick and creamy baked potato soup.

JALAPEÑO POPPER CORNBREAD

BREAD MACHINE SETTING: BASIC/WHITE PROGRAM

Frosty winter weather is no match for a big pot of chili and this spicy Jalapeño Popper Cornbread. This yeasted version from your bread machine is softer and more sliceable in a way that traditional cornbread just can't compare.

1½-POUND LOAF
1 cup (240 g) water
2 tsp (5 g) olive oil
2 tbsp (12 g) minced jalapeño
1 cup (80 g) shredded cheddar cheese
2¾ cups (376 g) bread flour
½ cup (61 g) self-rising yellow cornmeal (see Note)
2 tsp (8 g) sugar
¾ tsp (4.5 g) kosher salt
½ tsp (1 g) dried oregano or ½ tbsp (2 g) fresh oregano
1 tsp (3 g) yeast

2-POUND LOAF
1⅓ cups (320 g) water
1 tbsp (8 g) olive oil
3 tbsp (18 g) minced jalapeño
1½ cups (120 g) shredded cheddar cheese
3⅔ cups (501 g) bread flour
⅔ cup (81 g) self-rising yellow cornmeal (see Note)
1 tbsp (13 g) sugar
1 tsp (6 g) kosher salt
¾ tsp (2 g) dried oregano or 1 tbsp (4 g) fresh oregano
1¼ tsp (3.7 g) yeast

Add the ingredients to your bread machine's baking pan in the order they are listed, starting with the water and ending with the yeast.

Select the Basic/White program based on your machine's settings. Then select the coordinating setting for your loaf size on your machine and press Start.

When the loaf is done, remove it from the bread pan and transfer it to a wire rack to cool for at least 30 minutes before slicing.

NOTE: Self-rising yellow cornmeal has been ground to an especially fine texture and is not the same as regular cornmeal. You can find packages of it near the specialty flours section of your grocery store.

SERVING SUGGESTIONS

Slice and dunk in your favorite spicy chili topped with a dollop of sour cream and more shredded cheddar.

Serve alongside a Mexican pozole or chicken tortilla soup.

Toast slices and make an open-faced pulled pork sandwich with extra BBQ sauce.

CHAPTER 3

BREAKFAST TABLE TREATS

These sweet breakfast breads will encourage you to think beyond the toaster. While any one of them would be simply delicious sliced and served with a pat of butter, there are so many more ways to play with your food.

The classic Brioche (page 61) is your blank canvas for a wide variety of breakfast treats from French toast to fruity bread puddings. Try mixing cream cheese with your favorite spices or fruits and top a slice of The Best Banana Bread (page 65) or Aloha Pineapple Bread (page 75). You can also sandwich two slices of Maple Pecan (page 66) or Orange Chocolate Chip (page 81) bread with Nutella and griddle it up for a treat worthy of any dessert table.

BRIOCHE

BREAD MACHINE SETTING: SWEET PROGRAM

This light and fluffy and oh-so-buttery bread is the perfect addition to your breakfast table. It will hold up to whatever flavor combination you need it to match, from savory eggy casseroles to sweet homemade jams.

1½-POUND LOAF
¾ cup (180 g) water
5 tbsp (70 g) butter, softened and cut into pieces
1 large egg
3 cups (411 g) all-purpose flour
3 tbsp (37 g) sugar
1 tsp (6 g) kosher salt
1½ tsp (4.5 g) yeast

2-POUND LOAF
1 cup (240 g) water
8 tbsp (112 g) butter, softened and cut into pieces
1 large egg
4 cups (548 g) all-purpose flour
¼ cup (50 g) sugar
1¼ tsp (7.5 g) kosher salt
1¾ tsp (5.5 g) yeast

Add the ingredients to your bread machine's baking pan in the order they are listed, starting with the water and ending with the yeast.

Select the Sweet program setting on your machine and then select the coordinating setting for your loaf size and press Start. The Sweet setting helps to prevent burning the crust of the delicate loaf. If your machine doesn't have it, check your manual for how to bake a sweet bread. You could also use the Basic program on the lightest crust setting possible.

When the loaf is done, remove it from the bread pan and transfer it to a wire rack to cool for at least 30 minutes before slicing.

SERVING SUGGESTIONS

Use thick slices for mind-blowing French toast. Add some cinnamon to the batter and top with fresh berries.

Delicate brioche makes a wonderful base for a griddled croque madame breakfast sandwich made with sliced ham, cheese and a fried egg on top.

Toast and spread with cream cheese or ricotta and top with fresh sliced peaches and a sprinkle of blueberries.

LEMON BLUEBERRY BREAD

BREAD MACHINE SETTING: SWEET PROGRAM

This fresh-tasting sweet bread is similar to a brioche but with some zing. While the dough may appear soft in your machine, it will rise beautifully and bake up with a wonderfully light texture. Dried blueberries are essential since fresh berries would be beaten to a puree during the kneading phase. They'll rehydrate perfectly during the baking process. I love to buy them in a large, budget-friendly bag at Costco.

1½-POUND LOAF	2-POUND LOAF
¾ cup (185 g) sour cream	1 cup (246 g) sour cream
⅓ cup (82 g) buttermilk	½ cup (123 g) buttermilk
1 large egg plus 1 egg yolk	1 large egg plus 1 egg yolk
1 tbsp (15 g) lemon juice	1½ tbsp (22 g) lemon juice
1 tsp (2 g) lemon zest	1½ tsp (3 g) lemon zest
3 tbsp (42 g) butter, softened and cut into pieces	5 tbsp (70 g) butter, softened and cut into pieces
3 cups (411 g) bread flour	4 cups (548 g) bread flour
¼ cup (50 g) sugar	6 tbsp (75 g) sugar
1½ tsp (9 g) kosher salt	2 tsp (12 g) kosher salt
2½ tsp (7 g) yeast	3 tsp (9 g) yeast
MIX-INS	MIX-INS
½ cup (84 g) dried blueberries	¾ cup (126 g) dried blueberries

Add the ingredients to your bread machine's baking pan in the order they are listed, from the sour cream to the yeast. Reserve the blueberries.

Select the Sweet program on your machine. Then select the coordinating setting for your loaf size and press Start. The Sweet setting helps prevent burning the crust of the delicate loaf. If your machine doesn't have it, check your manual for how to bake a sweet bread or set a custom bake. You could also use the Basic program on the lightest crust setting possible.

Most machines will alert you with a beep when it is time to add the dried blueberries. If yours does not, add them in the middle of the second knead cycle.

When the loaf is done, transfer it to a wire rack to cool for at least 30 minutes before slicing.

SERVING SUGGESTIONS

Just a bit of butter is all you really need, but try these fun twists on toast:

- Ricotta, a drizzle of honey with a bit of lemon zest and fresh blueberries
- A dollop of lemon curd
- A thin spread of cream cheese and berries

THE BEST BANANA BREAD

BREAD MACHINE SETTING: BASIC/WHITE PROGRAM

When life gets stressful, bakers turn to banana bread for good reason. Warm and comforting, the heavenly aroma of cinnamon-spiced bananas baking soothes the soul. This yeasted version is easy to slice and is dotted with savory pecans for a bit of crunch. You'll find the loaf to be lighter and fluffier than your regular quick bread.

1½-POUND LOAF

⅓ cup (80 g) milk
½ cup (112 g) mashed ripe bananas (about 1½)
1 large egg
2 tbsp (28 g) butter, softened and cut into pieces
3 cups (411 g) bread flour
3 tbsp (37 g) sugar
¾ tsp (4.5 g) kosher salt
¼ tsp (0.7 g) cinnamon
1 tsp (3 g) yeast

MIX-INS
¾ cup (83 g) chopped pecans

2-POUND LOAF

½ cup (120 g) milk
⅔ cup (149 g) mashed ripe bananas (about 2)
1 large egg
2 tbsp (28 g) butter, softened and cut into pieces
4 cups (548 g) bread flour
¼ cup (50 g) sugar
1 tsp (6 g) kosher salt
½ tsp (1.3 g) cinnamon
1¼ tsp (3.7 g) yeast

MIX-INS
1 cup (109 g) chopped pecans

Add the ingredients to your bread machine's baking pan in the order they are listed, starting with the milk and ending with the yeast. Reserve the pecans for adding to the machine during the mix-in cycle.

Select the Basic/White program setting based on your machine's options. Then select the coordinating setting for your loaf size on your machine and press Start.

Most machines will alert you with a beep when it is time to add the pecans. If yours does not, add them to the machine in the middle of the second knead cycle.

When the loaf is done, remove it from the bread pan and transfer it to a wire rack to cool for at least 30 minutes before slicing.

SERVING SUGGESTIONS

Toast a slice and spread with peanut butter or a bit of Nutella and then top with fresh sliced bananas.

Make a simple sandwich with sweetened cream cheese and fresh fruit.

Cube and use in an overnight banana bread breakfast casserole.

MAPLE PECAN BREAD

BREAD MACHINE SETTING: BASIC/WHITE PROGRAM

Buttermilk powder gives a lovely chew to this slightly sweet maple bread, while chopped pecans bring the crunch. As a simple breakfast side or dressed up for a festive brunch, you'll turn to this classic flavor all year long.

1½-POUND LOAF

1 cup (240 g) water
2 tbsp (28 g) butter, melted
3 tbsp (60 g) maple syrup
3 cups (411 g) bread flour
⅓ cup (40 g) dry buttermilk powder
1½ tsp (9 g) kosher salt
1¾ tsp (5.5 g) yeast

MIX-INS
½ cup (55 g) chopped pecans

2-POUND LOAF

1½ cups (360 g) water
2 tbsp (28 g) butter, melted
¼ cup (80 g) maple syrup
4 cups (548 g) bread flour
½ cup (60 g) dry buttermilk powder
2 tsp (12 g) kosher salt
2¼ tsp (7 g) yeast

MIX-INS
¾ cup (84 g) chopped pecans

Add the ingredients to your bread machine's baking pan in the order they are listed, starting with the water and ending with the yeast. Place the chopped pecans in a separate bowl next to your machine or inside your machine's automatic nut dispenser if it has one.

Select the Basic/White program based on your machine's options. Then select the coordinating setting for your loaf size and press Start.

Most machines will alert you with a beep when it is time to add the nuts. If yours does not, add the nuts to the machine in the middle of the second knead cycle.

When the loaf is done, remove it from the bread pan and transfer it to a wire rack to cool for at least 30 minutes before slicing.

SERVING SUGGESTIONS

Pair with slices of peppered bacon and a fried egg for a unique sweet and salty breakfast sandwich.

Cut into triangles, toast under the broiler and serve alongside whipped strawberry cream cheese or a spicy sausage dip for a unique brunch dish.

Make a grilled chicken cordon bleu sandwich with slices of deli chicken, deli ham and slices of swiss cheese.

BLUEBERRY STREUSEL MUFFIN BREAD

BREAD MACHINE SETTING: BASIC/WHITE PROGRAM

The very best blueberry muffins are topped with a crispy brown sugar streusel.
This sweet breakfast bread has a similar streusel layered in with portions of dough and is
baked entirely in your bread machine for a unique treat. The layers will bake together into a
solid loaf, leaving your bread with a streusel swirl throughout each slice.

1½-POUND LOAF
¾ cup (180 g) milk
1 large egg
3 tbsp (45 g) water
2 tbsp (28 g) butter, softened and cut into pieces
3 cups (411 g) bread flour
3 tbsp (37 g) sugar
¾ tsp (4.5 g) kosher salt
¼ tsp (0.7 g) ground nutmeg
¼ tsp (1 g) orange zest or dried orange peel
1 tsp (3 g) yeast

MIX-INS
⅓ cup (55 g) dried blueberries

2-POUND LOAF
1 cup (240 g) milk
1 large egg
¼ cup (60 g) water
3 tbsp (42 g) butter, softened and cut into pieces
4 cups (548 g) bread flour
¼ cup (50 g) sugar
1 tsp (6 g) kosher salt
½ tsp (1.3 g) ground nutmeg
¼ tsp (1 g) orange zest or dried orange peel
1¼ tsp (3.7 g) yeast

MIX-INS
½ cup (60 g) dried blueberries

STREUSEL TOPPING
½ cup (69 g) all-purpose flour
⅓ cup (73 g) packed brown sugar
1 tsp (2.6 g) cinnamon
3 tbsp (42 g) butter, softened

(continued)

BLUEBERRY STREUSEL MUFFIN BREAD (CONT.)

Add the ingredients to your bread machine's baking pan in the order they are listed, starting with the milk and ending with the yeast. Reserve the blueberries for adding to the machine during the mix-in cycle.

Select the Basic/White program based on your machine's options. Then select the coordinating setting for your loaf size on your machine and press Start.

Most machines will alert you with a beep when it is time to add the blueberries. If yours does not, add them to the machine in the middle of the second knead cycle.

Prepare the streusel topping: While the bread is being kneaded, you will have enough time to prepare the streusel. Add the ingredients to a small bowl and mash them together with a fork, continuing to press and stir until the butter is completely incorporated into the flour. It is easiest to form the large clumps of streusel by using your fingers to pinch the mixture together at the end. Store the streusel in the fridge until it is needed.

After the second knead cycle is complete, transfer the dough from the bread pan to a baking mat. Remove the paddle. Working quickly, divide the dough into 10 to 12 pieces. Gently layer a few portions of dough back into the bread pan and sprinkle the prepared streusel over the top. Continue to add layers of dough and sprinkles of streusel until the pan is evenly filled. Sprinkle any remaining streusel over the top of the dough and return the bread pan to the machine to complete the final rise and bake cycles. There's no need to pause your machine as long as you get the pan back into place within 5 to 10 minutes.

When the loaf is done, gently remove it from the bread pan and transfer it to a wire rack to cool for at least 30 minutes before slicing.

SERVING SUGGESTIONS

You can also bake this bread as a regular loaf without the streusel, which makes it easier to slice for toast or cube for a bread pudding. A brown sugar cream cheese spread would be the perfect spread for a warm piece of toast.

APPLE CRISP BREAD

BREAD MACHINE SETTING: BASIC/WHITE PROGRAM

Juicy apples with a sweet brown sugar and oats swirl give this amazing bread a unique chewy texture with bits of crunch sprinkled throughout. It just might be one of the best ways to use up your orchard haul this fall.

1½-POUND LOAF
⅔ cup (160 g) milk
2 tbsp (30 g) apple juice
½ cup (55 g) peeled and chopped apple (I prefer Pink Ladies, Granny Smith or Honeycrisp)
1 large egg
1 tsp (2 g) orange zest
2 tbsp (28 g) butter, softened and cut into pieces
3 cups (411 g) bread flour
2 tbsp (25 g) sugar
¾ tsp (4.5g) kosher salt
½ tsp (1.3 g) cinnamon
1 tsp (3 g) yeast

2-POUND LOAF
⅔ cup (160 g) milk
2 tbsp (30 g) apple juice
⅔ cup (73 g) peeled and chopped apple (I prefer Pink Ladies, Granny Smith or Honeycrisp)
1 large egg
1½ tsp (3 g) orange zest
3 tbsp (42 g) butter, softened and cut into pieces
4 cups (548 g) bread flour
3 tbsp (37 g) sugar
1 tsp (6 g) kosher salt
¾ tsp (2 g) cinnamon
1¼ tsp (3.7 g) yeast

APPLE CRISP TOPPING
⅓ cup (46 g) all-purpose flour
⅓ cup (73 g) packed brown sugar
¼ cup (20 g) quick cooking oats
½ tsp (1.3 g) cinnamon
¼ tsp (0.7 g) nutmeg
2 tbsp (28 g) softened butter

(continued)

APPLE CRISP BREAD (CONT.)

Add the ingredients to your bread machine's baking pan in the order they are listed, starting with the milk and ending with the yeast.

Select the Basic/White program based on your machine's options. Then select the coordinating setting for your loaf size on your machine and press Start.

Prepare the apple crisp topping: Add the ingredients to a small bowl. Mash them together with a fork and continue to press and stir until the butter is completely incorporated into the flour. It is easiest to form large clumps of topping by using your fingers to pinch the mixture together.

After the second knead cycle is complete, transfer the dough from the bread pan to a baking mat. Remove the paddle. Divide the dough into 10 to 12 pieces. Gently layer a few portions of dough back into the bread pan and top with a sprinkle of the apple crisp topping. Continue to layer the dough and sprinkle the topping until your pan is evenly filled. Sprinkle any remaining topping mixture over the top of the dough and return the bread pan to the machine to complete the final rise and bake cycles. There is no need to pause your machine as long as you return the pan to the machine within 5 to 10 minutes.

When the loaf is done, gently remove it from the bread pan and transfer it to a wire rack to cool for at least 30 minutes before slicing.

SERVING SUGGESTIONS

This sweet bread is the perfect treat with a mug of hot apple cider or your favorite fall flavored coffee.

Slice into wedges and serve on a fall snack board with cheddar cheese, fresh apple slices and spiced pecans.

Griddle a slice in butter and drizzle with a bit of salted caramel sauce for an amazingly simple dessert.

ALOHA PINEAPPLE BREAD

BREAD MACHINE SETTING: BASIC/WHITE PROGRAM

Beat the winter doldrums with this sunshiny sweet bread that will have you dreaming of a tropical getaway. Pretty enough for a party but easy enough for your regular weekend brunch, slices of this pineapple bread hit the spot at every occasion.

1½-POUND LOAF
1 (6-oz [170-g]) can pineapple juice
2 tbsp (30 g) milk
2 tbsp (28 g) butter, melted
1½ tsp (6 g) vanilla
1 large egg
3 cups (411 g) bread flour
2 tbsp (25 g) sugar
¾ tsp (5 g) kosher salt
1 tsp (3 g) yeast

MIX-INS
½ cup (100 g) candied pineapple
½ cup (46 g) sweetened shredded coconut

2-POUND LOAF
1 (6-oz [170-g]) can pineapple juice
3 tbsp (45 g) milk
3 tbsp (42 g) butter, melted
1¾ tsp (7 g) vanilla
1 large egg
4 cups (548 g) bread flour
3 tbsp (37 g) sugar
1 tsp (6 g) kosher salt
1¼ tsp (4 g) yeast

MIX-INS
½ cup (100 g) candied pineapple
½ cup (46 g) sweetened shredded coconut

CRISPY COCONUT TOPPING
1 tbsp (14 g) butter, melted
¼ cup (23 g) sweetened shredded coconut

(continued)

ALOHA PINEAPPLE BREAD (CONT.)

Add the ingredients to your bread machine's baking pan in the order they are listed, starting with the pineapple juice and ending with the yeast. Reserve the candied pineapple and coconut for adding to the machine during the mix-in cycle.

Select the Basic/White program based on your machine's options. Then select the coordinating setting for your loaf size and press Start.

Roughly chop your candied pineapple so the pieces are no larger than a regular raisin or your machine will struggle to blend them in. Most machines will alert you with a beep when it is time to add the pineapple and coconut. If yours does not, add them to the machine in the middle of the second knead.

Prepare the topping: In a small bowl, stir together the melted butter and shredded coconut until everything is evenly coated. Sprinkle it over the top of the bread at the end of the third rise, before the bake cycle begins. The machine will not beep to alert you, so you may wish to check your bread machine manual for the cycle timing.

When the loaf is done, remove it from the bread pan and transfer it to a wire rack to cool for at least 30 minutes before slicing.

SERVING SUGGESTIONS

Slice the bread into squares and serve on a breakfast platter with fresh fruit and cream cheese dip.

Add to a brunch menu featuring brown sugar breakfast sausage and an egg scramble with peppers and onions.

Griddle slices in a pat of butter and top with vanilla ice cream.

CHOCOLATE ALMOND BREAD

BREAD MACHINE SETTING: SWEET PROGRAM

Is this a bread for breakfast or dessert? You decide! Life is short; eat the chocolate first.
The dash of espresso powder enhances the rich chocolatey taste without making the bread
taste like coffee. I keep a small jar in my pantry for adding to chocolate cakes and brownies,
but you can easily skip it if you prefer.

1½-POUND LOAF

¾ cup (180 g) milk

1 large egg

3 tbsp (42 g) butter, softened and cut into pieces

¾ tsp (3 g) almond extract

3 cups (411 g) bread flour

¼ cup (50 g) sugar

3 tbsp (18 g) unsweetened cocoa powder

1¼ tsp (7.5 g) kosher salt

½ tsp (1 g) instant espresso powder

2 tsp (6 g) yeast

MIX-INS

½ cup (85 g) semisweet chocolate chips

2-POUND LOAF

1 cup (240 g) milk

1 large egg

4 tbsp (56 g) butter, softened and cut into pieces

1 tsp (4 g) almond extract

4 cups (548 g) bread flour

⅓ cup (66 g) sugar

¼ cup (24 g) unsweetened cocoa powder

1¼ tsp (7.5 g) kosher salt

¾ tsp (1.5 g) instant espresso powder

2½ tsp (8 g) yeast

MIX-INS

⅔ cup (114 g) semisweet chocolate chips

(continued)

CHOCOLATE ALMOND BREAD (CONT.)

Add the ingredients to your bread machine's baking pan in the order they are listed, starting with the milk and ending with the yeast. Reserve the chocolate chips for adding to the machine during the mix-in cycle.

Select the Sweet program on your machine. Then select the coordinating setting for your loaf size and press Start. The Sweet setting helps prevent burning the crust of the delicate loaf. If your machine doesn't have it, check your manual for how to bake a sweet bread or set a custom bake. You could also use the Basic program on the lightest crust setting possible.

Most machines will alert you with a beep when it is time to add the chocolate chips. If yours does not, add them to the machine in the middle of the second knead.

When the loaf is done, remove it from the bread pan and transfer it to a wire rack to cool for at least 30 minutes before slicing.

SERVING SUGGESTIONS

This bread steals the show in any brunch or after-dinner coffee tray. Just add butter.

Cube and use for a memorable chocolate bread pudding.

Slice and griddle up sandwiches filled with cream cheese. Cut into triangles to serve.

ORANGE CHOCOLATE CHIP BREAD

BREAD MACHINE SETTING: SWEET PROGRAM

Whether you're squeezing fresh oranges during citrus season or just want to use up the last bit of juice from the bottle in your fridge, pairing bright orange with rich chocolate is a total win. The orange zest adds an extra burst of flavor, but if the fridge is running empty you can leave it out and try it next time.

1½-POUND LOAF	2-POUND LOAF
½ cup (125 g) orange juice	⅔ cup (166 g) orange juice
⅓ cup (80 g) milk	½ cup (120 g) milk
1 large egg	1 large egg
1 tbsp (6 g) orange zest	1 tbsp (6 g) orange zest
3 tbsp (42 g) butter, softened and cut into pieces	4 tbsp (56 g) butter, softened and cut into pieces
3 cups (411 g) bread flour	4 cups (548 g) bread flour
¼ cup (50 g) sugar	⅓ cup (66 g) sugar
2 tsp (5 g) cinnamon	1 tbsp (8 g) cinnamon
1¼ tsp (7.5 g) kosher salt	1½ tsp (9 g) kosher salt
2 tsp (6 g) yeast	2¼ tsp (7 g) yeast
MIX-INS	MIX-INS
⅓ cup (57 g) semisweet chocolate chips	½ cup (85 g) semisweet chocolate chips

Add the ingredients to your bread machine's baking pan in the order they are listed, starting with the orange juice and ending with the yeast. Reserve the chocolate chips for adding to the machine during the mix-in cycle.

Select the Sweet program on your machine. Then select the coordinating setting for your loaf size and press Start. The Sweet setting helps prevent burning the crust of the delicate loaf. If your machine doesn't have it, check your manual for how to bake a sweet bread or set a custom bake. You could also use the Basic program on the lightest crust setting possible.

Most machines will alert you with a beep when it is time to add the chocolate chips. If yours does not, add them to the machine in the middle of the second knead.

When the loaf is done, remove it from the bread pan and transfer it to a wire rack to cool for at least 30 minutes before slicing.

SERVING SUGGESTIONS

This bread makes a delicious weekday breakfast with a side of yogurt or your favorite eggs.

For a weekend brunch, serve this bread with mimosas, a frittata and spicy sausage.

Slice and toast several pieces under the broiler. Add to your holiday tea party tray with whipped butter and a chocolate cream cheese spread.

ALMOND CHERRY BREAD

BREAD MACHINE SETTING: BASIC/WHITE PROGRAM

No need to wait for cherry season to arrive! Dried cherries work much better than fresh fruit in this sweet loaf. The double dose of almond from the extract and almond butter gives a nutty flavor to each delicious bite. Individual packets of almond butter are just the right size to keep on hand for a 1½-pound loaf.

1½-POUND LOAF	2-POUND LOAF
1¼ cups (300 g) milk	1⅔ cups (400 g) milk
1 tsp (4 g) almond extract	1¼ tsp (5 g) almond extract
1 tbsp (14 g) butter, softened and cut into pieces	1½ tbsp (21 g) butter, softened and cut into pieces
2 tbsp (30 g) almond butter	3 tbsp (45 g) almond butter
3 cups (411 g) bread flour	4 cups (548 g) bread flour
3 tbsp (37 g) sugar	¼ cup (50 g) sugar
1½ tsp (9 g) kosher salt	1¾ tsp (11 g) kosher salt
2 tsp (6 g) yeast	2½ tsp (8 g) yeast
MIX-INS	MIX-INS
½ cup (60 g) dried cherries, roughly chopped	¾ cup (124 g) dried cherries, roughly chopped

Add the ingredients to your bread machine's baking pan in the order they are listed, starting with the milk and ending with the yeast. Reserve the dried cherries for adding to the machine during the mix-in cycle.

Select the Basic/White program based on your machine's options. Then select the coordinating setting for your loaf size on your machine and press Start.

Most machines will alert you with a beep when it is time to add the dried cherries. If yours does not, add them to the machine in the middle of the second knead.

When the loaf is done, remove it from the bread pan and transfer it to a wire rack to cool for at least 30 minutes before slicing.

SERVING SUGGESTIONS

Slice and serve as part of a hot cocoa snack tray in the winter.

Make a slice of toast, spread with ricotta cheese and top with chopped roasted almonds or a sprinkle of mini chocolate chips.

Cut into chunks and serve as part of a snack board with Swiss, white cheddar or goat cheese and roasted almonds.

CHAPTER 4

HOLIDAY CELEBRATIONS

Looking for something a little extra special to round out your festive holiday menu? You're sure to find the perfect flavor for any seasonal celebration among these easy, hands-off breads. Bonus: They'll save you crucial time for cooking the rest of your feast.

Toast the end of the year with a slice of the Hot Buttered Rum (page 88) or Spiced Eggnog & Pear (page 92) bread that will help you ring in the merriest of seasons. The Savory Stuffing Bread (page 91) will come in handy when you want the ultimate Thanksgiving leftovers sandwich. And in spring, enjoy a simple Sweet Carrot Cake (page 103) or Poppy Seed Tea (page 107) bread for your holiday brunch. Whatever your loved ones are celebrating, you're sure to find the perfect match here.

WARM & COZY PUMPKIN BREAD

BREAD MACHINE SETTING: BASIC/WHITE PROGRAM

This yeasted version of the popular fall quick bread has a much lighter texture and is far easier to slice. It will fit right into your toaster without falling apart. Be sure to try a warm and crispy slice with a bit of butter and cinnamon sugar.

1½-POUND LOAF
½ cup (120 g) milk
⅓ cup (82 g) pure pumpkin puree
¼ cup (60 g) water
1 large egg
1½ tbsp (21 g) butter, softened and cut into pieces
3 cups (411 g) bread flour
¾ tsp (4.5 g) kosher salt
½ tsp (1.3 g) pumpkin pie spice
1 tsp (3 g) yeast

2-POUND LOAF
⅔ cup (160 g) milk
½ cup (122 g) pure pumpkin puree
⅓ cup (80 g) water
1 large egg
2 tbsp (28 g) butter, softened and cut into pieces
4 cups (548 g) bread flour
1 tsp (6 g) kosher salt
¾ tsp (2 g) pumpkin pie spice
1¼ tsp (3.7 g) yeast

Add the ingredients to your bread machine's baking pan in the order they are listed, starting with the milk and ending with the yeast.

Select the Basic/White program based on your machine's options. Then select the coordinating setting for your loaf size and press Start.

When the loaf is done, remove it from the bread pan and transfer it to a wire rack to cool for at least 30 minutes before slicing.

SERVING SUGGESTIONS

Slice it up and serve with a fall fruit salad featuring chopped crispy apples, sweet grapes and crunchy pecans for an easy weekday breakfast.

Layer slices with an egg custard for an overnight French toast casserole and bake it the next morning. Serve the French toast casserole with hot apple cider for a weekend brunch.

Cube and make a pumpkin bread pudding with salted caramel sauce drizzled over the top.

HOT BUTTERED RUM BREAD

BREAD MACHINE SETTING: BASIC/WHITE PROGRAM

Stoke the fireplace, pour a hot toddy and nibble on this sweet loaf when the winter chill is nipping at your toes. Just the aroma of this festive bread baking in your machine will warm you through and through.

1½-POUND LOAF
¾ cup (180 g) milk
¼ cup (60 g) water
4 tbsp (56 g) butter, melted
1 tbsp (15 g) rum
3 cups (411 g) bread flour
2 tbsp (28 g) packed brown sugar
½ tsp (1.3 g) cinnamon
⅛ tsp (0.3 g) nutmeg
⅛ tsp (0.3 g) cloves
¾ tsp (4.5 g) kosher salt
1 tsp (3 g) yeast

2-POUND LOAF
1 cup (240 g) milk
⅓ cup (80 g) water
5 tbsp (70 g) butter, melted
2 tbsp (30 g) rum
4 cups (548 g) bread flour
3 tbsp (42 g) packed brown sugar
1 tsp (3 g) cinnamon
¼ tsp (0.6 g) nutmeg
¼ tsp (0.6 g) cloves
1 tsp (6 g) kosher salt
1¼ tsp (3.7 g) yeast

BUTTERED RUM GLAZE
¼ cup (30 g) powdered sugar
1 tbsp (14 g) butter, melted
½ tsp (8 g) rum or rum extract (optional)

Add the ingredients to your bread machine's baking pan in the order they are listed, starting with the milk and ending with the yeast.

Select the Basic/White program based on your machine's options. Then select the coordinating setting for your loaf size and press Start.

Just before the bread is finished with the baking cycle, prepare the glaze: Add the powdered sugar, half of the melted butter and the rum to a small mixing bowl. Stir them together with a fork and continue to drizzle in just enough melted butter to reach the consistency you desire. A thicker glaze will let you pipe on a decorative drizzle and a thinner glaze will spread more evenly.

When the bread is finished baking, transfer it to a wire rack over parchment paper. Let the bread cool slightly before spreading the glaze over the top.

SERVING SUGGESTIONS

Pair this loaf with a bundle of mulling spices and apple cider for a thoughtful neighbor gift.

Take a break from the holiday hustle for a coffee date with friends. You bring the bread, they bring the lattes.

SAVORY STUFFING BREAD

BREAD MACHINE SETTING: BASIC/WHITE PROGRAM

Fill your home with the delicious smells of Thanksgiving all in one bread pan. This deliciously seasoned bread is the easiest way to elevate your turkey dinner, either as an actual stuffing side dish or for leftover sandwiches all weekend long.

1½-POUND LOAF	2-POUND LOAF
⅓ cup (53 g) finely chopped onion	½ cup (80 g) finely chopped onion
1 cup (240 g) milk	1¼ cups (300 g) milk
3 tbsp (45 g) water	3 tbsp (45 g) water
1½ tbsp (21 g) butter, softened and cut into pieces	2 tbsp (28 g) butter, softened and cut into pieces
3 cups (411 g) bread flour	4 cups (548 g) bread flour
2 tsp (8 g) sugar	1 tbsp (12.5 g) sugar
2 tsp (5 g) poultry seasoning	1 tbsp (8 g) poultry seasoning
¾ tsp (4.5 g) kosher salt	1 tsp (6 g) kosher salt
1 tsp (3 g) yeast	1¼ tsp (3.7 g) yeast

Add the ingredients to your bread machine's baking pan in the order they are listed, starting with the onion and ending with the yeast. The onions will add moisture to the dough and bake into the bread and should be added with the liquids and not during the mix-in phase during kneading.

Select the Basic/White program based on your machine's options. Then select the coordinating setting for your loaf size and press Start.

When the loaf is done, remove it from the bread pan and transfer it to a wire rack to cool for at least 30 minutes before slicing.

SERVING SUGGESTIONS

Layer slices of turkey and cranberry sauce and top with delicious melted brie on thick slices for the best Thanksgiving leftovers sandwich ever.

Cube the entire loaf and make dried croutons for a stuffing with built-in flavor.

Toast and cut into fingers for dunking in leftover gravy.

SPICED EGGNOG & PEAR BREAD

BREAD MACHINE SETTING: BASIC/WHITE PROGRAM

On the first day of Christmas, give your true love this delicately sweet pear bread, no partridge required. Save your sweet and juicy ripe pears for this recipe and watch them practically dissolve into the sweet dough.

1½-POUND LOAF	2-POUND LOAF
½ cup (120 g) prepared eggnog	¾ cup (180 g) prepared eggnog
¼ cup (60 g) water	¼ cup (60 g) water
½ cup (80 g) peeled and minced ripe pear (about ½ of a large pear)	¾ cup (120 g) peeled and minced ripe pear (about ¾ of a large pear)
1 large egg	1 large egg
2 tbsp (28 g) butter, softened and cut into pieces	3 tbsp (42 g) butter, softened and cut into pieces
1 tbsp (15 g) Amaretto (optional—add 1 tbsp [15 g] of eggnog if you prefer)	1 tbsp (15 g) Amaretto (optional—add 1 tbsp [15 g] of eggnog if you prefer)
3 cups + 3 tbsp (437 g) bread flour	4¼ cups (582 g) bread flour
2 tbsp (25 g) sugar	3 tbsp (37 g) sugar
¾ tsp (4.5 g) kosher salt	1 tsp (6 g) kosher salt
¼ tsp (0.7 g) ground nutmeg	½ tsp (1.3 g) ground nutmeg
1¼ tsp (3.7 g) yeast	1½ tsp (4.5 g) yeast

Add the ingredients to your bread machine's baking pan in the order they are listed, starting with the eggnog and ending with the yeast. The pears will add moisture to the dough and bake into the bread and should be added with the liquids and not during the mix-in phase during kneading.

Select the Basic/White program based on your machine's options. Then select the coordinating setting for your loaf size on your machine and press Start.

When the loaf is done, remove it from the bread pan and transfer it to a wire rack to cool for at least 30 minutes before slicing.

SERVING SUGGESTIONS

Slice and serve alongside fresh fruit with whipped butter for a simple Christmas morning treat.

Slice several pieces, spread with butter and sprinkle with cinnamon sugar and toast in an even layer under the broiler for a big batch of the best cinnamon toast ever.

Cube and use in a holiday bread pudding with dried cranberries and eggnog glaze.

CRANBERRY & WHITE CHOCOLATE DELIGHT

BREAD MACHINE SETTING: BASIC/WHITE PROGRAM

The coffeehouse can keep their dense cranberry bars—this light and delicate bread is a much more perfect pairing for your morning latte during the holiday season. Bright and cheery cranberries make each slice festive with hints of white chocolate chips that practically melt into the dough for a touch of sweetness.

1½-POUND LOAF
¾ cup (180 g) water
2 large eggs
3 tbsp (24 g) vegetable oil
1 tsp (4 g) vanilla
3 cups (411 g) bread flour
1½ tsp (9 g) kosher salt
1 tbsp (12.5 g) sugar
1¾ tsp (5.5 g) yeast

MIX-INS
½ cup (84 g) dried sweetened cranberries
½ cup (85 g) white chocolate chips

2-POUND LOAF
1 cup (240 g) water
2 large eggs
¼ cup (33 g) vegetable oil
1½ tsp (6 g) vanilla
4 cups (548 g) bread flour
2 tsp (12 g) kosher salt
1½ tbsp (18.8 g) sugar
2 tsp (6 g) yeast

MIX-INS
¾ cup (124 g) dried sweetened cranberries
¾ cup (127 g) white chocolate chips

(continued)

CRANBERRY & WHITE CHOCOLATE DELIGHT (CONT.)

Add the ingredients to your bread machine's baking pan in the order they are listed, starting with the water and ending with the yeast. Reserve the dried cranberries and white chocolate chips for adding to the machine during the mix-in cycle.

Select the Basic/White program based on your machine's options. Then select the coordinating setting for your loaf size on your machine and press Start.

Most machines will alert you with a beep when it is time to add the dried cranberries and white chocolate chips. If yours does not, add them to the machine in the middle of the second knead cycle.

When the loaf is done, remove it from the bread pan and transfer it to a wire rack to cool for at least 30 minutes before slicing.

SERVING SUGGESTIONS

Make a festive French toast and drizzle with a simple syrup made from orange juice instead of maple syrup.

Cube and use in an overnight breakfast casserole with cream cheese glaze and chopped almonds for a sweet Christmas morning breakfast.

Get a loaf started in the morning while you decorate your home for the holidays. Enjoy the sweet smells while you work and reward yourself with a slice when you're done.

IT'S NOT A FRUITCAKE BREAD

BREAD MACHINE SETTING: SWEET PROGRAM

Sit back, Grandma, we've got this one. Fruitcake gets a bad rap during the holidays but when you use a custom mix of quality candied fruits and nuts, you get a hearty bread filled with delicious sweet bites. You can mix up a custom combination of candied orange, candied lemon, golden raisins and dried cranberries or use a premade blend. We love the prepared "Yuletide Cheer Fruit Blend" from King Arthur Baking mixed with chopped hazelnuts. A little buttered rum glaze from page 88 over the top wouldn't hurt either!

1½-POUND LOAF	2-POUND LOAF
1 cup + 2 tbsp (270 g) milk	1⅓ cups (320 g) milk
1 egg yolk	1 egg yolk
3 cups (411 g) bread flour	4 cups (548 g) bread flour
2 tbsp (25 g) sugar	3 tbsp (37 g) sugar
1½ tsp (9 g) kosher salt	2 tsp (12 g) kosher salt
½ tsp (1.3 g) cinnamon	¾ tsp (2 g) cinnamon
¼ tsp (0.7 g) nutmeg	½ tsp (1 g) nutmeg
¼ tsp (0.7 g) ginger	½ tsp (1 g) ginger
⅛ tsp (0.3 g) cloves	¼ tsp (0.6 g) cloves
2 tsp (6 g) yeast	2½ tsp (7.5 g) yeast
MIX-INS	MIX-INS
¾ cup (124 g) mixed dried fruits and nuts, chopped	1 cup (165 g) mixed dried fruits and nuts, chopped

(continued)

IT'S NOT A FRUITCAKE BREAD (CONT.)

Add the ingredients to your bread machine's baking pan in the order they are listed, starting with the milk and ending with the yeast. Reserve the dried fruitcake mix for adding to the machine during the mix-in cycle.

Select the Sweet program on your machine. Then select the coordinating setting for your loaf size on your machine and press Start. The Sweet setting helps prevent burning the crust of the delicate loaf. If your machine doesn't have it, check your manual for how to bake a sweet bread or set a custom bake. You could also use the Basic program on the lightest crust setting possible.

Most machines will alert you with a beep when it is time to add the fruitcake mix. If yours does not, add it to the machine in the middle of the second knead cycle.

When the loaf is done, remove it from the bread pan and transfer it to a wire rack to cool for at least 30 minutes before slicing.

SERVING SUGGESTIONS

This hearty bread is not overly sweet and pairs extremely well with a homemade coffee bar for holiday entertaining.

Bake a loaf and add a bow to a bottle of wine for a thoughtful gift for the class teacher, your co-worker gift exchange or your favorite neighbor.

Serve as a unique side dish for any cozy holiday brunch or after-dinner treat all December long.

CLASSIC HUMMINGBIRD BREAD

BREAD MACHINE SETTING: BASIC/WHITE PROGRAM

All the delicious flavors from *Southern Living*'s most popular cake for over forty years are featured in this rich, sweet loaf. Drizzle the cream cheese glaze and sprinkle a few pecans over the top for a stunning springtime holiday brunch.

1½-POUND LOAF	2-POUND LOAF
½ cup (123 g) buttermilk	⅔ cup (164 g) buttermilk
½ cup (112 g) mashed ripe banana	⅔ cup (150 g) mashed ripe banana
1 large egg	1 large egg
1 tbsp (14 g) butter, softened and cut into pieces	1½ tbsp (21 g) butter, softened and cut into pieces
1 tsp (4 g) vanilla	1½ tsp (6 g) vanilla
3 cups (411 g) bread flour	4 cups (548 g) bread flour
3 tbsp (37 g) sugar	¼ cup (50 g) sugar
½ tsp (1.3 g) cinnamon	¾ tsp (2 g) cinnamon
¾ tsp (4.5 g) kosher salt	1 tsp (6 g) kosher salt
1 tsp (3 g) yeast	1¼ tsp (3.7 g) yeast

MIX-INS

¼ cup (50 g) candied pineapple, chopped	⅓ cup (63 g) candied pineapple, chopped
¼ cup (28 g) chopped pecans	⅓ cup (36 g) chopped pecans

CREAM CHEESE GLAZE

¼ cup (2 oz [56 g]) cream cheese, softened

2 tbsp (15 g) powdered sugar

4–5 tsp (20–25 g) milk

(continued)

CLASSIC HUMMINGBIRD BREAD (CONT.)

Add the ingredients to your bread machine's baking pan in the order they are listed, starting with the buttermilk and ending with the yeast. Reserve the chopped pineapple and pecans for adding to the machine during the mix-in cycle.

Select the Basic/White program based on your machine's options. Then select the coordinating setting for your loaf size and press Start.

Most machines will alert you with a beep when it is time to add the pineapple and pecans. If yours does not, add them to the machine in the middle of the second knead.

When the bread is finished baking, remove it from the bread pan and transfer to a wire rack over a piece of parchment paper. Let the bread cool slightly while you prepare the glaze.

To prepare the glaze: Add the cream cheese and powdered sugar to a small bowl. Whisk them together until they are combined. Add the milk 1 teaspoon at a time until your desired consistency is reached. A thicker glaze will let you pipe on a pattern and a thinner one will spread evenly over the top.

Spread or pipe the glaze over the top of the bread and sprinkle additional chopped pecans as desired. Alternatively, you can double the glaze recipe and serve it alongside the bread with a spreader knife to let guests spread it over slices of bread for even more delicious coverage.

SERVING SUGGESTIONS

Prepare a loaf ahead for Mother's Day for the easiest breakfast-in-bed with coffee.

Slice and serve with sweet tea for a southern-style wedding or bridal shower.

Serve with a savory brunch featuring poached eggs, hollandaise sauce and fresh asparagus.

SWEET CARROT CAKE BREAD

BREAD MACHINE SETTING: BASIC/WHITE PROGRAM

Don't wait for Easter morning to enjoy this easy carrot cake bread—your family will enjoy this sweet treat all spring long. Be sure to shred your own fresh carrots rather than buying pre-shredded from the store because they'll bake into the dough better and give a smoother texture.

1½-POUND LOAF

1 (8-oz [225-g]) can crushed pineapple, undrained

⅓ cup (37 g) shredded carrot

1 large egg

1 tsp (4 g) vanilla

2 tbsp (28 g) butter, softened and cut into pieces

3 cups (411 g) bread flour

2 tbsp (25 g) sugar

¾ tsp (4.5 g) kosher salt

1 tsp (2.6 g) cinnamon

1 tsp (3 g) yeast

2-POUND LOAF

1 (8-oz [225-g]) can crushed pineapple, undrained

½ cup (55 g) shredded carrot

1 large egg

1½ tsp (6 g) vanilla

3 tbsp (42 g) butter, softened and cut into pieces

4 cups (548 g) bread flour

3 tbsp (37 g) sugar

1 tsp (6 g) kosher salt

1½ tsp (4 g) cinnamon

1¼ tsp (3.7 g) yeast

CREAM CHEESE GLAZE

¼ cup (2 oz [56 g]) cream cheese, softened

2 tbsp (15 g) powdered sugar

1 tsp (4 g) vanilla

4–5 tsp (20–25 g) milk

(continued)

SWEET CARROT CAKE BREAD (CONT.)

Add the ingredients to your bread machine's baking pan in the order they are listed, starting with the pineapple and ending with the yeast.

Select the Basic/White program based on your machine's options. Then select the coordinating setting for your loaf size and press Start.

When the bread is finished baking, remove it from the bread pan and transfer it to a wire rack over a piece of parchment paper. Let the bread cool slightly while you prepare the glaze.

To prepare the glaze: Add the cream cheese and powdered sugar to a mixing bowl. Beat them together with a mixer until they are combined. Add the vanilla and 2 teapoons (10 g) of milk and beat them together until smooth and slightly runny. Add additional milk 1 teaspoon at a time until you achieve your desired consistency. A thicker glaze will let you pipe on a decorative drizzle and a thinner glaze will spread more evenly.

Spread the glaze over the slightly warm bread if you want it to melt into an even coating. If you prefer to pipe a decorative pattern, you'll want to wait for the bread to completely cool first.

SERVING SUGGESTIONS

Serve slices of this bread with wedges of fresh pineapple alongside a bowl of tangy cream cheese fruit dip.

Skip the glaze and make cream cheese sandwiches, cut into bite-sized squares and add to a tea table for a holiday brunch.

Use for a unique "stuffed" French toast filled with whipped cream cheese and chopped pecans or golden raisins.

POPPY SEED TEA BREAD

BREAD MACHINE SETTING: BASIC/WHITE PROGRAM

Lightly scented with a bit of lemon zest, this delicately sweet bread is the perfect partner for your coffee or teatime. The sour cream gives the loaf a substantial texture that makes for easy slicing.

1½-POUND LOAF

⅔ cup (160 g) milk
⅓ cup (82 g) sour cream
1 large egg
1 tbsp (6 g) lemon zest
3 tbsp (42 g) butter, softened and cut into pieces
3 cups (411 g) bread flour
¼ cup (50 g) sugar
2 tbsp (17 g) poppy seeds
¾ tsp (4.5 g) kosher salt
1 tsp (3 g) yeast

2-POUND LOAF

¾ cup (180 g) milk
½ cup (123 g) sour cream
1 large egg
1½ tbsp (9 g) lemon zest
4 tbsp (56 g) butter, softened and cut into pieces
4 cups (548 g) bread flour
⅓ cup (66 g) sugar
3 tbsp (24 g) poppy seeds
1 tsp (6 g) kosher salt
1¼ tsp (3.7 g) yeast

Add the ingredients to your bread machine's baking pan in the order they are listed, starting with the milk and ending with the yeast.

Select the Basic/White program based on your machine's options. Then select the coordinating setting for your loaf size and press Start.

When the loaf is done, remove it from the bread pan and transfer it to a wire rack to cool for at least 30 minutes before slicing.

SERVING SUGGESTIONS

Slice the bread and use cookie cutters to trim simple shapes. Griddle them in a bit of butter and top with lemon curd and fresh strawberries.

Make sweet finger sandwiches by layering two slices with whipped strawberry butter and cutting into squares.

Assemble a sweet snack board for teatime with toasted slices cut into dunker strips served alongside fresh blackberries and candied almonds.

LUCK OF THE IRISH SODA BREAD

BREAD MACHINE SETTING: BASIC/ WHITE PROGRAM

Your day is sure to be lucky when it starts off with a warm slice of this classic Irish bread. The buttermilk helps give an excellent crust and chew to each piece while a touch of orange zest freshens up the entire loaf. Can't find currants at your store? You can substitute raisins, but chop them so they are about a quarter of their regular size.

1½-POUND LOAF

1 cup (245 g) buttermilk

1 large egg

3 tbsp (42 g) butter, softened and cut into pieces

1 tsp (2 g) orange zest

3 cups (411 g) all-purpose flour

3 tbsp (37 g) sugar

¾ tsp (3.5 g) baking soda

1 tsp (6 g) kosher salt

1 tsp (3 g) yeast

MIX-INS

¾ cup (124 g) dried currants

2-POUND LOAF

1¼ cups (306 g) buttermilk

1 large egg

4 tbsp (56 g) butter, softened and cut into pieces

1 tsp (2 g) orange zest

4 cups (548 g) all-purpose flour

¼ cup (50 g) sugar

1 tsp (4.6 g) baking soda

1¼ tsp (7.5 g) kosher salt

1¼ tsp (3.7 g) yeast

MIX-INS

1 cup (165 g) dried currants

Add the ingredients to your bread machine's baking pan in the order they are listed, starting with the buttermilk and ending with the yeast. Reserve the dried currants for adding to the machine during the mix-in cycle.

Select the Basic/White program based on your machine's options. Then select the coordinating setting for your loaf size and press Start.

Most machines will alert you with a beep when it is time to add the currants. If yours does not, add them to the machine in the middle of the second knead.

When the loaf is done, remove it from the bread pan and transfer it to a wire rack to cool for at least 30 minutes before slicing.

SERVING SUGGESTIONS

Serve as a side dish for your St. Patrick's Day feast with Irish stew and cabbage.

Serve thick slices with softened butter as a side for a breakfast of eggs and corned beef hash.

Dip slices into a thick and creamy Irish potato and leek soup.

CHAPTER 5

FUN WITH DOUGH

One of my family's favorite features of bread machines is the ability to make a gorgeous hands-off dough for a special treat baked in the oven. You can easily turn any one of the recipes in this book into an oven-baked bread—see the full instructions on the very next page! But if you want to feel like a kid again playing with soft, buttery dough, these playful yet practical recipes will fit your meal planning needs perfectly.

Roll up your sleeves and grab a rolling pin. You're going to love the smells of warm, fresh Classic Cinnamon Rolls (page 123) or the sweet Hot Cross Buns (page 115) baking in your kitchen.

Do you want to absolutely wow your friends at your next party? Make the Epic Party Pretzel Platter (page 133) and watch the tasty pretzels disappear in a flash. If you've got kids, they will have a blast rolling out the dough snakes for the homemade soft pretzels.

Do you want something more interactive for spaghetti night? Don't miss the Garlic Pull-Apart Bread (page 121) or the warm slices of Fluffy Focaccia (page 127) for dunking into that savory tomato sauce.

I invite you to think beyond the bread pan and whip up something tasty with my favorite kitchen shortcut—your bread machine.

HOW TO BAKE A TRADITIONAL LOAF IN YOUR OVEN

The all-in-one feature of the bread machine makes bread making so convenient for busy bakers, but it is truly just the tip of the iceberg of what can be done with your machine.

Why would you want to make dough in your machine only to bake it in the oven?

- You desire a more traditional bread loaf shape without the paddle causing any issues.

- You're excited to play with twists, braids or shaped breads.

- Your meal plan would benefit from individual homemade rolls instead of a loaf.

Any of the previous loaf recipes in this book can be tweaked for baking in the oven.

Step 1: Choose the loaf size you want.

For the 1½-pound loaf, you'll need two 8 x 5–inch (20 x 13–cm) bread pans.

For the 2-pound loaf, you'll need two 9 x 6–inch (23 x 15–cm) bread pans.

Step 2: Use the Dough program.

Load your bread pan as the recipe suggests but choose the Dough program instead of the Baking program recommended. If your recipe includes mix-ins, know that most machines will not beep for the mix-in phase on the Dough program. There is only one long kneading cycle on the Dough program, so simply watch your dough and wait until the ball has been thoroughly mixed. Add the mix-ins once the machine is vigorously beating the dough ball and watch it to be sure they get fully incorporated.

Step 3: Divide the dough in half.

When the dough cycle is finished, transfer the dough to a baking mat coated in a sprinkle of all-purpose flour. You may need to help ease the dough out of the pan with your hands if it sticks to the sides of the bread pan. Remove the paddle attachment and divide the dough into two equal portions using a knife or dough scraper. You may want to weigh the portions on a food scale to be sure they are even.

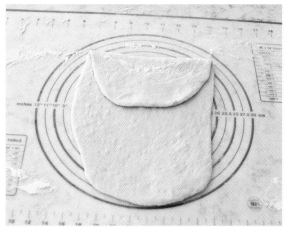

With the narrow end of the dough facing you, fold the top edge down ⅓ toward the center of the dough.

Fold the bottom edge up toward the center, overlapping the first fold.

Turn the dough so the folded edges face you.

Fold the top edge down ⅓ toward the center.

Fold the bottom edge up toward the center, overlapping the first fold. Pinch and seal the seam.

Place the bread seam side down in a greased bread pan. Cover with plastic wrap and let rise for 30 to 60 minutes or until the bread just reaches the top edge of the pan.

Step 4: Pat one section of the dough into a rectangle.

Simply use your hands to pat one portion of dough out at a time until it is ½ inch (1.3 cm) thick. The narrow side of the rectangle should face you.

Step 5: Triple-fold the dough.

This step will help the bread form a beautiful, traditional loaf shape.

Starting with the narrow edge of the rectangle farthest away from you, fold the dough toward your body about a third of the way toward the center of the dough.

Fold the bottom edge of the dough up, overlapping the fold you just finished and lining up the edge of the bottom with the new top edge.

Turn the dough 90 degrees, then roll the dough up in a log shape and pinch the seam closed.

Repeat with the other portion of dough.

Step 6: Grease your baking pans and transfer the dough.

Spray a light coat of cooking oil or spread softened butter all around the inside of your two baking pans.

Transfer one portion of dough to each pan, placing it seam side down. Gently pat the dough into place, as it won't completely fill the bottom of the pan. Repeat with the other dough.

Cover the pans with plastic wrap and let the loaves rise for 30 minutes to an hour or until the center of the dough has reached just past the top edge of the baking pans.

Step 7: Bake the bread.

This step will require a little bit of experimentation based on the recipe you chose. A good rule of thumb to follow is:

Recipes that have a water base and no mix-ins: Preheat the oven to 400°F (204°C).

Recipes that include milk, a lot of butter or whole wheat flour: Preheat the oven to 350°F (177°C).

Bake the bread for 30 minutes and then check for doneness. The internal temperature should be around 190 to 205°F (88 to 96°C). Add additional baking time as needed for crust color and temperature. Use the accompanying photo with your recipe as a good gauge for the crust color for your bread. Some develop a much deeper color than others. If you discover your bread is browning too quickly and it hasn't yet reached the right internal temperature, tent the loaf with a bit of aluminum foil and continue to bake.

HOT CROSS BUNS

BREAD MACHINE SETTING: DOUGH PROGRAM

One a penny, two a penny? Grab your piggy bank—you're definitely going to want to take two of these classic Easter buns. They actually make a delicious sweet roll any time of the year. Light and fluffy with a wonderful chew, they will forever ruin you from buying the grocery store variety.

DOUGH FOR 12 BUNS
¾ cup (180 g) warm water
3 tbsp (42 g) butter, softened and cut into pieces
1 egg + 1 egg white
2⅔ cups (360 g) all-purpose flour
1 tbsp (7.5 g) buttermilk powder
¼ cup (50 g) sugar
1 tsp (2.6 g) cinnamon
½ tsp (3 g) kosher salt
1 tsp (3 g) yeast

MIX-INS
¾ cup (124 g) dried currants

EGG WASH
1 egg
1 tbsp (15 g) water

VANILLA GLAZE FOR CROSSES
½ cup (60 g) powdered sugar
3–4 tsp (15–20 g) milk

Add the ingredients to your bread machine's baking pan in the order they are listed, starting with the water and ending with the yeast. Reserve the currants for the mix-in cycle.

Select the Dough program on your machine and press Start.

Most bread machines will not beep when it is time to add the mix-ins on the Dough program. Simply watch for the dough ball to form completely. Once the machine starts to vigorously beat the dough, add the currants and watch to ensure that they are fully incorporated. You can help knead them in a bit more when you form the rolls.

If you notice the dough is sticking too much to the pan during the kneading phase, add 1 to 2 tablespoons (8.5 to 17 g) of additional flour as needed.

When the dough is finished, transfer it to a lightly floured baking mat. You may have to ease the dough out of the pan with your hands. Scoop up any dough that is stuck inside and add it to the dough on your mat. Remove the paddle and punch the dough down. Let it rest for 10 minutes.

Meanwhile, grease a 9 x 13–inch (23 x 33–cm) pan with softened butter. Preheat the oven to 375°F (190°C). When the dough is done resting, pat it into a rough rectangular shape for easier portioning. Use a bench scraper tool or knife to cut the dough into 12 equal pieces.

(continued)

HOT CROSS BUNS (CONT.)

Working one portion of dough at a time, shape smooth, round rolls by folding the sides of the dough up under the bottom. Place them evenly in the baking pan in three rows of four and cover with plastic wrap. Let the rolls rise for 1 hour or until they are doubled in size.

Beat the egg and water together with a fork to make the egg wash. Brush it over the top of the buns. Bake them for 18 to 20 minutes, or until the tops are lightly toasted and the internal temperature reads 200°F (93°C). Watch that the buns don't get over toasted at the end of the cooking time. You can cover them lightly with aluminum foil to prevent over-browning.

When the buns are finished baking, let them rest in the pan for 5 minutes and then transfer them to a wire rack to cool completely before frosting them.

To form the traditional hot cross bun crosses: Whisk together the powdered sugar and milk until you have a slightly thickened consistency. Add the glaze to a ziplock baggie and snip a small corner from the bag. You'll have more frosting than you need for the crosses, but this helps make the piping squeeze more easily from your piping bag.

TIPS FOR MAKING AHEAD: You can bake the rolls a day in advance, let them cool completely and store in an airtight container or bread box. You can also freeze fully baked rolls for up to 3 months and simply thaw them overnight. In either case, reserve the final frosting decoration for the day you want to serve them.

SERVING SUGGESTIONS

Traditionally served for Easter dinner, these rolls would be delicious for any springtime holiday meal.

Skip the frosting top and instead slice and toast them open-face under the broiler. Try topping them with whipped cream cheese or your favorite sweetened butter.

Pair them with any spring menu featuring ham, fish, a light salad or soup.

BUTTERY DINNER ROLLS

BREAD MACHINE SETTING: DOUGH PROGRAM

These buttery soft, savory dinner rolls bring a restaurant-quality bread basket to your dinner table. Square-folded rolls are easy to split open and slather with a sweet honey butter that melts right into the fluffy bread. If you want something a little different, try adding a pinch of cayenne to the honey butter recipe for a spicy kick!

DOUGH FOR 15 ROLLS

1 cup (240 g) milk
1 large egg
1 tbsp (14 g) butter, softened and cut into pieces
3 cups (411 g) all-purpose flour
⅓ cup (73 g) packed brown sugar
1 tsp (6 g) kosher salt
1 tbsp (9 g) yeast

TOPPING

2 tbsp (28 g) butter, melted, for brushing over baked rolls

TIPS FOR MAKING AHEAD: Leftover rolls can last up to 3 days if you reheat them in the oven for 3 to 5 minutes to restore their texture. Frozen, fully baked rolls can be thawed overnight and then reheated before serving if you want to make them ahead of a holiday or special dinner.

SERVING SUGGESTIONS

Whip together 8 tablespoons (112 g) of softened butter and ¼ cup (85 g) of honey with 1 teaspoon (2 g) of cinnamon for serving with warm rolls.

These buns are perfectly sized for making mini ham and cheese sliders.

Pile up a platter of dinner rolls to serve with your favorite chicken salad.

Add the ingredients to your bread machine's baking pan in the order they are listed, starting with the milk and ending with the yeast.

Select the Dough program on your machine and press Start.

Grease a 9 x 13–inch (23 x 33–cm) pan with softened butter. Transfer the dough to a baking mat coated with a sprinkle of all-purpose flour. Remove the paddle and roll the dough into about an 11 x 14–inch (28 x 35–cm) rectangular shape. Use a bench scraper tool or knife to cut the dough into 15 equal square pieces.

Working one portion of dough at a time, fold each square in half and place in three rows of five buns in your prepared pan. The finished pan will look better if all the folds are facing in the same direction. If you prefer, you can shape smooth, round rolls by folding the sides of the dough up under the bottom. Cover the pan with plastic wrap. Let the rolls rise for 25 to 35 minutes or until they are doubled in size.

Preheat the oven to 350°F (177°C). Remove the plastic wrap and bake the rolls for 8 to 12 minutes, or until the tops are lightly toasted and the internal temperature reads 190°F (88°C). If the rolls are browning too quickly, lightly cover them with aluminum foil while they finish baking. Brush the rolls with melted butter and serve them warm.

GARLIC PULL-APART BREAD

BREAD MACHINE SETTING: DOUGH PROGRAM

This fun bubble bread makes your average spaghetti night spectacular.
Simply serve the loaf on a platter at the table and let everyone pass and
pull their favorite pieces—no knives needed!

DOUGH FOR 1 PULL-APART BREAD

¾ cup (180 g) milk

3 tbsp (42 g) butter, softened and cut into pieces

1 large egg

3 cups (411 g) all-purpose flour

1 tbsp (12.5 g) sugar

1 tsp (6 g) kosher salt

2 tsp (6 g) yeast

GARLIC FILLING

6 tbsp (84 g) butter, melted

2 tbsp (12.5 g) grated Parmesan cheese

2 tsp (5 g) minced garlic

2 tsp (5 g) Italian herb blend

¼–½ tsp (0.7–1.3 g) crushed red pepper flakes

Add the dough ingredients to your bread machine's baking pan in the order listed, from the milk to the yeast. Reserve the filling ingredients for when you assemble the pull-apart bread.

Select the Dough program setting and press Start. As the dough kneads, it will initially appear very dry and shaggy but should form a nice ball after the end of the knead cycle.

When the bread machine is finished, remove the dough from the bread pan and place it on a lightly floured baking mat. Remove the paddle and divide the dough into 16 to 20 pieces. Each piece of dough will become one of the pull-apart pieces. Gently form them into rough ball shapes; there's no need to worry about them being perfectly uniform. They make the bread even more fun to pull apart at the table.

Grease a 9 x 6–inch (23 x 15–cm) bread pan with softened butter and assemble the garlic filling. In a small bowl, combine all the filling ingredients and stir together with a spoon.

(continued)

GARLIC PULL-APART BREAD (CONT.)

Lightly place some of the dough balls into the pan in a single layer, avoiding tightly packing them. Drizzle a fourth of the buttery garlic filling over the top. Add another layer of dough balls, then drizzle with another fourth of the garlic filling. Add the last layer of dough and pour another fourth of garlic filling over the top. Reserve the final fourth of the garlic filling for just before baking. Cover and let rise for 30 minutes or until the rolls look nice and puffed up but not quite doubled in size.

Preheat the oven to 350°F (177°C). Drizzle the last fourth of the garlic filling over the top just before baking. Place the bread pan on a larger cookie sheet to catch any runaway portions of dough and bake for 30 to 40 minutes or until golden brown. This bread is best served warm.

SERVING SUGGESTIONS

This interactive loaf is way more fun than garlic bread and is perfect for serving with your favorite pasta dinner. Dip a piece into tomato sauce, serve it with a Caesar salad or enjoy as an appetizer with a bottle of wine and an Italian-themed snack board.

CLASSIC CINNAMON ROLLS

BREAD MACHINE SETTING: DOUGH PROGRAM

Ooey-gooey cinnamon and brown sugar filling surrounded by the most perfect light and chewy sweetened dough is an amazing way to start your morning. Just add a drizzle of icing and a cup of coffee.

DOUGH FOR 12 ROLLS

1¼ cups (300 g) milk
1 tsp (4 g) vanilla
3 tbsp (42 g) butter, softened and cut into pieces
3 cups (411 g) all-purpose flour
3 tbsp (37 g) sugar
1¼ tsp (8 g) kosher salt
2 tsp (6 g) yeast

FOR THE FILLING

3 tbsp (42 g) butter, melted
½ cup (110 g) packed brown sugar
1 tbsp (7 g) cinnamon

FOR THE ICING

1 cup (120 g) powdered sugar
1 tbsp (14 g) butter, melted
1 tsp (4 g) vanilla
2 tbsp (30 g) milk

Add the ingredients to your bread machine's baking pan in the order they are listed, starting with the milk and ending with the yeast.

Select the Dough program on your machine and press Start.

When the dough is finished, remove it from the bread pan and transfer it to a lightly floured baking mat. Remove the paddle and sprinkle the top of the dough with a little more flour. Gently pat it into a rectangular shape for easier rolling and then let it rest while you prepare the baking pan.

Spread a 9 x 13–inch (23 x 33–cm) baking pan with softened butter and then prepare the filling. Mix together the melted butter, brown sugar and cinnamon. It will be very thick and almost paste-like, which will make it much easier to spread. Set it aside while you roll the dough.

Flour a rolling pin and roll the dough out to a roughly 12 x 15–inch (30 x 38–cm) rectangle. The longer edge should be facing you. If you are struggling to get an even shape with your rolling pin, use your floured hands to gently pat the corners of the dough until they are squared off. An oval-shaped dough will not cut evenly on the ends.

Use a combination of a frosting spreader tool and your fingers to spread the prepared filling mixture all over the dough from the left edge to the right edge and from the long edge facing you to 1 inch (2.5 cm) away from the long edge furthest from you. The filling should cover three sides of dough, leaving just the 1-inch (2.5-cm) border furthest from you.

(continued)

CLASSIC CINNAMON ROLLS (CONT.)

Starting at the long end of the dough closest to you, roll up the dough until you have a tight rolled log. You can use your hands to gently pat each end to make the rolls more even before you slice the log.

Use a knife or bench scraper tool to cut the log into 12 equal pieces and lay them cut-side up in the prepared baking dish. Cover the pan with plastic wrap and let the rolls rise for 20 to 30 minutes or until they are nearly doubled in size.

Meanwhile, preheat the oven to 375°F (190°C). Bake the rolls for 20 to 25 minutes or until the tops are lightly toasted. If the tops are browning too quickly, lightly cover the pan with aluminum foil and continue to bake until the dough at the center of the rolls no longer looks wet and shiny and is firm when you gently wiggle the center of the pinwheel.

Prepare the icing: Whisk together the powdered sugar, melted butter, vanilla and milk until the mixture is smooth. Drizzle all over the top of the warm cinnamon rolls and serve.

TIPS FOR MAKING AHEAD: To have fresh cinnamon rolls for an early breakfast, assemble the rolls in the pan the day before. Cover them with plastic wrap and place in the refrigerator for 8 to 24 hours ahead of baking. In the morning, let them rise on the counter for an hour and then bake as directed.

SERVING SUGGESTIONS

Prepare these cinnamon rolls ahead of time and let them rise on the counter while you open gifts on Christmas morning or while the kids hunt for eggs on Easter. They make a perfect and easy addition to your holiday brunch.

Split the recipe into two 8 x 8–inch (20 x 20–cm) pans and give prepared, unbaked rolls with finishing instructions as gifts during the holiday season.

Channel your inner Midwesterner and serve cinnamon rolls with spicy chili. It's totally a thing.

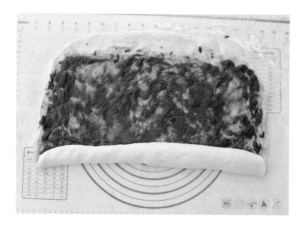

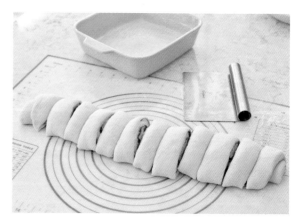

FLUFFY FOCACCIA

BREAD MACHINE SETTING: DOUGH PROGRAM

If making dough in your machine and baking it in the oven worries you, this is the perfect recipe to start with because you simply pat the dough out into a pan and bake it— no roll forming required.

DOUGH FOR 1 (9 X 13–INCH [23 X 33–CM])
FOCACCIA

1 cup + 2 tbsp (270 g) water, room temperature
2 tbsp + 1 tsp (20 g) olive oil
3 cups + 2 tbsp (428 g) bread flour
½ tsp (2 g) sugar
2 tsp (5 g) Italian herb blend
1 tsp (6 g) kosher salt
1½ tsp (4.5 g) yeast

TOPPINGS

4–5 tbsp (32–40 g) olive oil, divided
2 tbsp (3 g) fresh rosemary, chopped
Sprinkle of fresh cracked peppercorn

SERVING SUGGESTIONS

Fluffier than traditional focaccia, you can serve this bread as a dipper for pasta night.

Drizzle a few tablespoons (24 g) of olive oil into a shallow plate and add a sprinkle of grated Parmesan cheese, red pepper flakes, fresh cracked pepper and a dash of balsamic vinegar for a tasty appetizer with a glass of red wine.

Simply search "focaccia garden" and prepare to have your mind blown by the gorgeous scenes you can make out of vegetables and herbs before baking.

Add the ingredients to your bread machine's baking pan in the order listed, starting with the water and ending with the yeast.

Choose the Dough program on your machine and press Start.

When the dough cycle is finished, remove the dough from the bread pan and place it on a lightly floured baking mat. Remove the paddle and punch down the dough to deflate it. Let the dough rest for 10 minutes. Meanwhile, brush a 9 x 13–inch (23 x 33–cm) shallow rimmed baking pan with 2 tablespoons (16 g) of olive oil.

Roll the dough out to a roughly 9 x 13–inch (23 x 33–cm) shape and transfer it to the pan. If the dough keeps shrinking back into a smaller shape, let it rest for a few minutes and try again. You may find it easier to pat it into place directly in the pan. Cover it with plastic wrap and let it rise for 40 to 50 minutes. It should puff up evenly but not quite double in size.

Pour a generous 2 to 3 tablespoons (16 g to 24 g) of olive oil over the top of the dough and use your fingers to rub it all over the surface. Gently press your fingertips into the top to make ½-inch (1.3-cm)-deep indentations roughly 1 inch (2.5 cm) apart, all across the top. Sprinkle the fresh herbs and pepper evenly over the top.

Preheat the oven to 450°F (232°C). Bake for 13 to 15 minutes or until lightly golden brown. Be careful—it can overcook quickly so it needs to be watched for the final minutes.

CLASSIC PRETZEL TWISTS

BREAD MACHINE SETTING: DOUGH PROGRAM

Crispy on the outside, chewy on the inside, these hot, soft pretzels beat any snack you've ever had at a ballgame. This salty original is our favorite, but don't miss the fun flavor swaps and dip ideas on page 133.

DOUGH FOR 16 PRETZELS

1 cup (240 g) milk

1 tbsp (14 g) butter, melted

3 cups (411 g) bread flour

2 tbsp (28 g) packed brown sugar

¾ tsp (4.5 g) kosher salt

1¼ tsp (3.7 g) yeast

FOR THE WATER BATH

½ cup (110 g) baking soda

9 cups (2.2 kg) water

TOPPING

Kosher salt

Add the ingredients to your bread machine's baking pan in the order listed, starting with the milk and ending with the yeast.

Choose the Dough program on your machine and press Start.

When the bread machine is finished, remove the dough from the pan and place it on a baking mat. Do not flour the mat; you want the dough to remain slightly sticky so that the pretzels are easier to roll. Remove the paddle.

Prepare a shallow rimmed baking pan with parchment paper and preheat the oven to 400°F (204°C).

Use a knife or bench scraper tool to divide the dough into 16 equal portions. To prevent your dough from drying out while you form each pretzel one at a time, you may wish to dampen some fresh paper towels or a clean tea towel and cover the resting dough while you work.

Roll out each ball of dough to form a 16-inch (40-cm) rope. Shape the pretzel by crossing over the ends to form a circle with two tails and pull the tails down toward you. Twist the tails once and tuck them under the bottom edge of the circle. Gently press the tips into place to hold the shape and set the pretzel on the lined baking pan. See page 131 for step-by-step photos. Repeat with the remaining portions of dough.

(continued)

CLASSIC PRETZEL TWISTS (CONT.)

Prepare the water bath: Add the baking soda to the water in a medium- to large-sized pot. Whisk it together and then bring to a boil. Do not dump the entire portion of baking soda to already boiling water or it will immediately bubble up over the sides of the pan and onto your stovetop and could cause a burn to your hand. If you forgot to add the baking soda and the water is already boiling, just carefully sprinkle in a little at a time and wait for the fizz to dissipate before adding more baking soda. Using a slotted spoon, dunk each pretzel, just one or two at a time, into the water bath for 20 to 30 seconds. They will rise to the top of the water quickly and you can gently tap them back under the water but it isn't necessary. Scoop the pretzels out of the water with your slotted spoon, drain and place them back on the prepared baking sheet. Immediately sprinkle the top with a pinch of Kosher salt. Repeat until all the pretzels are prepared.

Bake for 8 to 12 minutes, or until the pretzels are lightly golden brown.

SERVING SUGGESTIONS

Cut the dough "snakes" into 1½-inch (4-cm) nuggets for homemade pretzel bites.

Use classic salted pretzels for a taste test of several fun or new-to-you condiments.

Make an entire party platter with a variety of flavors for sampling—check out the delicious ideas on page 133.

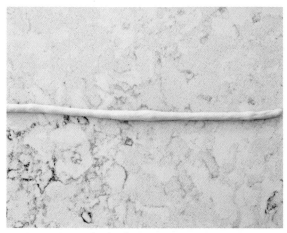

Roll out a 16-inch (40-cm) rope.

Cross over the two ends to form a circle with two tails.

Pull the tails down toward you to form a knot.

Twist the tails around each other and press to seal against the bottom.

Dip the pretzel in the water bath for 20 to 30 seconds.

Place on a baking sheet and immediately sprinkle with kosher salt.

CLASSIC SALTED PRETZELS
WITH HONEY MUSTARD

ALMOND CRUNCH
WITH NUTELLA DIP

GARLIC PARMESAN
WITH WARM
MARINARA

CINNAMON
SUGAR WITH
STRAWBERRY
CREAM CHEESE
DIP

JALAPEÑO POPPY
SEED WITH WARM
QUESO

EPIC PARTY PRETZEL PLATTER

10 DELICIOUSLY FUN WAYS TO PLAY WITH YOUR HOMEMADE PRETZELS

No matter how old your party guests might be, everyone will feel like a kid again when they dig into this jaw-dropping snack board. Mix a few sweet and savory options together with an assortment of deliciously easy dips and let your friends dip and dunk to their hearts' content. You can mix a variety of options on just one baking pan using the flavored toppings or plan ahead and make a batch or two of different flavored doughs.

PLAY WITH THE TOPPINGS

Assemble a pan of classic pretzels from page 128 and simply skip the sprinkle of kosher salt over the top. With just 2 tablespoons (28 g) of melted butter, you can flavor one pan of plain pretzels with a variety of these fun recipes for a sampler that makes a fun and easy party platter.

Cinnamon Sugar: Brush unsalted baked pretzels with melted butter. Sprinkle cinnamon sugar over the entire surface and serve warm.

Fun Dip Idea: Strawberry cream cheese

Almond Crunch: Combine ½ cup (54 g) of slivered almonds with 2 tablespoons (25 g) of sugar in a food processor. Pulse until the almonds are in small pieces. Add the assembled pretzels to the water bath and then brush them with melted butter, sprinkle the almond mixture over the top and bake as directed. They may need a few more minutes to bake so that the nut mixture gets a nice toasted color on top.

Fun Dip Idea: Nutella

Garlic Parmesan: Brush unsalted baked pretzels with melted butter. Sprinkle them with a bit of garlic salt and then dip them into a plate of grated Parmesan cheese. Shake off the excess and serve warm.

Fun Dip Idea: Warm marinara sauce

Spicy Ranch: Brush unsalted baked pretzels with melted butter. Dip them in a plate of your favorite powdered ranch seasoning mixed with half a teaspoon of crushed red pepper flakes.

Fun Dip Idea: Warm marinara sauce

Honey Mustard: Mix together 3 tablespoons (63 g) of honey, 1 teaspoon (2.1 g) of ground dried mustard and 1 teaspoon (2.3 g) of onion powder. Brush the mixture over the top of the formed pretzels before baking.

Fun Dip Idea: Raspberry preserves

PLAY WITH THE DOUGH

Plan ahead for when you want to play with these flavors since they call for simple swaps to the classic dough recipe.

Cinnamon Orange: Add 2 teaspoons (4 g) of orange zest and ¾ teaspoon (2 g) of cinnamon to the other dough ingredients, just after the flour, then complete the pretzels as directed.

Fun Dip Idea: Cream cheese frosting

Pumpkin Spice: Add 1 teaspoon (2.6 g) of pumpkin spice blend to the other dough ingredients, just after the flour, then complete the pretzels as directed.

Fun Dip Idea: Pumpkin butter or salted caramel sauce

Honey Sriracha: Substitute 2 tablespoons (42 g) of honey for the sugar and add 1 teaspoon (6.5 g) of Sriracha sauce to the other dough ingredients and bake as directed.

Fun Dip Idea: Melted butter

Cranberry Spice: Add ½ teaspoon (1.3 g) of cinnamon and ¼ teaspoon (0.7 g) of nutmeg to the other dough ingredients, just after the flour. Add ½ cup (55 g) of dried cranberries during the mix-in phase.

Fun Dip Idea: Spicy mustard

Jalapeño Poppy Seed: Mince half a jalapeño with seeds and ribs removed and add it to the dough during the mix-in phase. Brush baked pretzels with melted butter and sprinkle poppy seeds over the top.

Fun Dip Idea: Warm queso

4 FLAVORS FROM JUST 1 BATCH!

| ALMOND CRUNCH | CINNAMON SUGAR | JALAPEÑO POPPY SEED | GARLIC PARMESAN |

TIM'S BUNS
THE PERFECT SOURDOUGH ROLL
BREAD MACHINE SETTING: DOUGH PROGRAM

Looking for hot bun perfection? My husband took it upon himself to test dozens of sourdough dinner rolls and we finally settled on these deliciously chewy buns. They hold up to the heartiest of sandwich fillings—sliced beef tenderloin is our personal favorite. For tips on getting started with sourdough, check out page 153.

DOUGH FOR 12 ROLLS

½ cup (100 g) sourdough starter
1 cup (240 g) water
⅓ cup (80 g) milk
2½ cups (360 g) bread flour
1 cup (137 g) all-purpose flour
2 tbsp (25 g) sugar
1½ tsp (9 g) kosher salt
1¼ tsp (3.7 g) yeast

TIPS FOR MAKING AHEAD: Leftover rolls can last up to 3 days if you reheat them in the oven for 3 to 5 minutes to restore their texture. They can even be sliced in half and toasted on the Bagel setting in your toaster.

Frozen rolls can be thawed overnight and then reheated before serving if you want to bake them ahead of a holiday or special dinner.

SERVING SUGGESTIONS

These delicious buns are perfect for any mini sandwich that has lots of chew: sliced beef, pulled pork or thick slices of leftover ham or turkey.

Toasted and spread with butter, they are great for a small fried egg sandwich.

Rip and dunk them in spicy beef chili and stews.

Add the ingredients to your bread machine's baking pan in the order they are listed, starting with the sourdough starter and ending with the yeast.

Select the Dough program on your machine and press Start.

When the dough is finished, remove it from the bread pan and transfer it to a lightly floured baking mat. You may need to use your hands to ease the dough out of the pan if it sticks. Remove the paddle and gently pat the dough into a rough rectangular shape for easier portioning. Use a bench scraper tool or knife to cut the dough into 12 equal pieces.

Line a baking sheet with parchment paper. Working one portion of dough at a time, shape smooth, round rolls by folding the sides of the dough up under the bottom and pinching the seam together. Place them evenly on the baking sheet, seam side down, and cover with plastic wrap. Let the rolls rise for 1 hour or until they have nearly doubled in size.

Preheat the oven to 400°F (204°C). Bake the rolls for 10 to 12 minutes or until the tops are lightly toasted and the internal temperature reads 200°F (93°C).

STRAWBERRY CREAM CHEESE SWIRLS

BREAD MACHINE SETTING: DOUGH PROGRAM

If a fruit or cheese Danish is your favorite bakery breakfast treat, you won't want to miss this easier strawberry swirl roll. Fresh strawberries are mixed with delicious jam and topped with cream cheese frosting for a new take on Classic Cinnamon Rolls (page 123).

DOUGH FOR 12 ROLLS

1¼ cups (300 g) milk

1 tsp (4 g) vanilla

3 tbsp (42 g) butter, softened and cut into pieces

3 cup (411 g) all-purpose flour

3 tbsp (37 g) sugar

1¼ tsp (7.5 g) kosher salt

2 tsp (6 g) yeast

FOR THE FILLING

½ cup (160 g) strawberry jam (We love the easy home-made freezer jam from The Ultimate Kid's Baking Book.)

¾ cup (125 g) strawberries, fresh or thawed from frozen, chopped

FOR THE CREAM CHEESE FROSTING

½ cup (4 oz [112 g]) cream cheese, softened

3 tbsp (42 g) butter, softened

1 tsp (4 g) vanilla

1½ cups (180 g) powdered sugar

Add the ingredients to your bread machine's baking pan in the order they are listed, starting with the milk and ending with the yeast.

Select the Dough program on your machine and press Start.

When the dough is finished, remove it from the bread pan and transfer it to a lightly floured baking mat. Remove the paddle and sprinkle the top of the dough with a little more flour. Gently pat it into a rectangular shape for easier rolling and then let it rest while you prepare the baking pan and chop the fresh strawberries.

Spread a 9 x 13–inch (23 x 33–cm) baking pan with softened butter.

Flour a rolling pin and roll the dough out to a roughly 12 x 15–inch (30 x 38–cm) rectangle. The longer edge should be facing you. If you are struggling to get an even shape with your rolling pin, use your floured hands to gently pat the corners of the dough until they are squared off. An oval-shaped dough will not cut evenly on the ends.

(continued)

STRAWBERRY CREAM CHEESE SWIRLS (CONT.)

Spread the strawberry jam all over the dough from the left edge to the right edge and from the long edge facing you to 1 inch away from the long edge furthest from you. The filling should cover three sides of dough, leaving just the 1-inch (2.5-cm) border furthest from you. Sprinkle the fresh strawberries evenly over the top of the jam.

Starting at the long end of the dough closest to you, roll up the dough until you have a tight rolled log. You can use your hands to gently pat each end to make the rolls more even before you slice the log.

Use a knife or bench scraper tool to cut the log into 12 equal pieces and lay them cut-side up in the prepared dish. You can tuck any berries that fell out during the transfer process into the layers of the rolls. Cover the pan with plastic wrap and let the rolls rise for 20 to 30 minutes or until they are nearly doubled in size.

Meanwhile, preheat the oven to 375°F (190°C). Remove the plastic wrap and cover the pan with aluminum foil. Bake the rolls for 25 to 30 minutes or until the tops are lightly toasted. After 10 minutes of baking, remove the foil so the tops can brown.

Prepare the cream cheese frosting: Beat together the cream cheese and butter until smooth. Mix in the vanilla until combined. Add the powdered sugar and beat until smooth and fluffy. Spread the frosting all over the top of the warm cinnamon rolls and serve.

SERVING SUGGESTIONS

These delicious rolls are perfect during the height of berry season in the summer but you can use thawed frozen strawberries in place of the fresh berries any time of year. A raspberry or blackberry variation would be an easy way to play with this recipe, too.

Serve these party-pretty rolls at a bridal or baby shower. They'd also make a fun and festive Valentine's Day surprise for your sweetie.

CARAMEL PECAN BREAKFAST BUNS

BREAD MACHINE SETTING: DOUGH PROGRAM

Not ready to jump into a cinnamon roll but want something extra special for brunch? These caramel pecan sticky buns are so addictive you may be tempted to keep the pan all to yourself. A little maple syrup in the dough makes the entire bun breakfast-y in every bite.

DOUGH FOR 12 BUNS

¾ cup (180 g) milk
¼ cup (56 g) butter, softened and cut into pieces
1 large egg
2 tbsp (40 g) maple syrup
3 cups (411 g) bread flour
2 tbsp (25 g) sugar
¼ tsp (1.5 g) kosher salt
1½ tsp (4.5 g) yeast

FOR THE CARAMEL

⅓ cup (75 g) butter
1 cup (220 g) packed brown sugar
¼ cup (85 g) light corn syrup
1 cup (109 g) chopped pecans

Add the ingredients to your bread machine's baking pan in the order they are listed, starting with the milk and ending with the yeast.

Select the Dough program on your machine and press Start.

Meanwhile, spread a 9 x 13–inch (23 x 33–cm) baking pan with softened butter. Just before the dough is finished, prepare the caramel filling. In a small saucepan, combine the butter, brown sugar and corn syrup and heat over low heat. Stir it constantly and watch for the first bubbles that signal the mixture is going to boil. Cook for 1 minute more and then pour the caramel immediately into the bottom of the prepared pan. Spread evenly across the bottom with a spatula, sprinkle the nuts evenly across and set aside.

Transfer the dough to a lightly floured baking mat. Remove the paddle and gently pat the dough into a rectangular shape for easy cutting. Divide the dough into 12 equal pieces. Round each portion into a bun by folding the sides of the dough up under the bottom and pinching the seam together. Line them up in the prepared pan in three rows of four, seam side down. Cover the pan with plastic wrap and let the buns rise for 45 minutes or until they have nearly doubled in size.

(continued)

CARAMEL PECAN BREAKFAST BUNS (CONT.)

Preheat the oven to 350°F (177°C). Bake the buns for 15 to 20 minutes or until the tops of the rolls are golden brown. If they are browning too quickly, you may wish to tent the pan with aluminum foil after 10 minutes of baking. Let the buns cool in the pan for just 2 minutes.

Run a clean knife around the edge of the pan to help release the buns. Place a piece of parchment paper a few inches longer than the pan on your counter. Place a wire rack over the pan and, while using oven mitts to protect your hands, pinch together the rack and the pan and flip the pan upside down over the parchment paper to catch drips of caramel. Firmly tap the pan with oven mitts to help release the nuts before carefully lifting the pan up. Let the caramel topping cool for 10 minutes to prevent burning your mouth or fingers and then serve warm.

These buns are best within the first 24 hours of baking, if they last that long. If you make them the day before, a 10-second spin in the microwave will warm them up just right, but the caramel will remain perfectly chewy at room temperature, too.

SERVING SUGGESTIONS

Think beyond just breakfast—these deliciously sticky buns make a surprising side dish for spicy BBQ dinners with pulled pork and veggies.

Pair the sweet caramel and pecans with a savory chicken and crisp apple salad.

Warm up your dinner by adding a pan of these rolls as a fun side dish for a spicy sweet potato and ginger soup.

CHAPTER 6

HOW DOES THIS THING WORK EXACTLY?

If you've already baked your first bread and have questions, I've got answers.

If you haven't dug in yet and don't even know what you don't know, I'm excited to help you, too.

In the coming pages, I'll answer common questions from new bread bakers and give you a tour of the totally practical machine you've got sitting on your counter. Get a bake or two under your belt and you're going to be utterly hooked.

COMMON QUESTIONS FROM NEWBIE BREAD BAKERS

How did your first bread turn out? Don't panic if it wasn't exactly perfect. We can fix it.

Now that you have a better feel for how your machine works, let's talk about expectations and troubleshoot together.

What kind of breads can I expect from my bread machine?

If you've been drooling over gorgeous artisan loaves on Instagram and are now staring at a less gorgeous brown loaf from your machine, it is important to recognize that a bread baked in a bread machine is a different creature than a bread baked in an oven.

Bread machine breads may not always be the most beautiful, but they are amazingly delicious and exceedingly practical. Real life is busy and fresh bread can easily be part of your family's regular dinner menu with this magical time-saving tool.

Once you've tried a recipe or two, you'll find that bread machine breads:

- Are softer overall and have slightly thicker crusts than other breads you've tried
- Offer consistent and predictable results from bread to bread in terms of shape and size
- Fit your toaster perfectly when sliced
- Rarely last longer than a day when served warm with softened butter at the family dinner table

If you're here hoping to bake breads with:

- Crispy crusts
- Braids, twists, boules and other fancy shapes
- Huge air holes from long rises with artisan doughs

Then you will want to use your bread machine as a practical tool for making dough that you finish in your oven. Be sure to check out Chapter 5 (page 111) for recipes that will let you play with your dough. The Fluffy Focaccia (page 127) or the Buttery Dinner Rolls (page 118) are perfect places to start.

What kind of flour should I use in my bread machine?

Most bread machine recipes will call for bread flour, which has a higher protein content than all-purpose flour. The extra protein gives a nicer rise to your dough. However, if you run out of bread flour, all-purpose can be substituted in a pinch. For best results, be sure to buy unbleached flour so that it has the right elements to feed your yeast. Bleached flour has the yeast's favorite things removed and is especially harmful to sourdough starter.

Our favorite brand by far is King Arthur Baking. You can find King Arthur bread flour and all-purpose flour at most major grocery chains in North America. If you don't have it available locally, they have wonderful shipping options for home bakers on their website.

Storage: Store your flour in an air-tight container. There is no reason to chill the flour in your fridge or freezer.

Why should I make dough in a bread machine if I plan to bake the recipe in the oven?

Even though my kitchen is outfitted with a stand mixer, a hand mixer and a good old-fashioned whisk, I highly prefer to make bread dough in my bread machine because I can simply dump the ingredients in, press a button and walk away.

The bread machine will knead the dough at just the right intervals and it provides a perfectly warm and toasty place for the dough to rise without interruption. It is so fun to come back to the kitchen and discover a fluffy mountain of perfect dough waiting for you.

What's the deal with the 1½-pound and 2-pound ingredients lists?

Most bread machines offer the option for baking more than one size of bread loaves. The loaf size needs to be selected before you even add ingredients to the pan so that you use the correct measurements. Select the matching setting on your machine since it will affect the rise and bake time of the loaf.

The loaf sizes are determined by the weight of all the ingredients, but the main difference is the flour:

·   1½-pound loaves: Use 3 cups of flour

·   2-pound loaves: Use 4 cups of flour

The pound setting for your loaf does not always guarantee a certain size in the final bread. You'll quickly discover that some bread recipes result in a higher rise than others, even at the same loaf size.

If your machine says it has a 2-pound capacity, you will still find that some of the 1½-pound recipes fill your entire bread pan. A 2-pound version of that same recipe would completely overflow your machine. To prevent this, always test the 1½-pound version of the recipe first.

Even if your machine offers a 2-pound or higher capacity, I firmly believe that the 1½-pound size is the most practical for most recipes. Two-pound loaves tend to rise and bake in unwieldy shapes, making slicing difficult. They don't fit in toasters nearly as nicely as the smaller loaves do. Personally, I'd much rather bake two 1½-pound loaves than one 2-pound loaf. The exception to this rule is breads baked in the Zojirushi "Home Bakery Supreme" bread machine, which only works with a 2-pound loaf. The bread pan is longer and thinner than other models I tested and forms a more practically sized 2-pound loaf.

However, if your plan is to cube the bread and make croutons, stuffing or bread pudding, you may appreciate the larger quantity of bread and not be worried about the size and shape of each individual slice. To give you that option and total flexibility, I've included both sizes for each of the recipes.

Why does the bread shape in the picture not match the bread I just made?

Any difference in the shape of the loaves likely comes down to which bread machine you own.

Various bread machines feature two different kinds of bread pans:

·   Horizontal bread pans
    This is the most common bread pan shape. Breville, Zojirushi and Hamilton Beach models all currently feature pans that let the top of the loaf rise upwards while the paddle attachment is inserted in the bottom center of the bread. Your resulting loaf will look most like a bread you buy at the store or that you bake in a regular oven.

·   Vertical bread pans
    The Cuisinart compact bread machine features a vertical bread pan that forces the loaf to create an even shape throughout. The paddle is inserted in one end of the bread while the other end is where the dough rises. Once you remove the loaf from the pan, turn the bread on its side to slice. You'll find every slice is uniform from end to end, which makes for excellent, even sandwiches.

If the slice featured in a photo is perfectly square with a slight clover appearance, it was baked in a Cuisinart machine. More traditional looking slices were baked in a Breville, Zojirushi or our 15-year-old Breadman Pro machine.

The darn paddle ripped a huge hole out of the center of my baked bread. How do I fix this?

The paddle is essential to the mixing and kneading of your bread but can definitely be a nuisance when it comes to the baking cycle and finished loaf. If you don't want to pull the paddle out of your pretty baked bread before serving, you'll want to remove it before the bake cycle even begins.

Many bread machines have an alert sound that tells you when it is safe to remove the paddle. If your machine doesn't have an automatic alarm, you can remove the paddle at the start of the third rise—that is, right after the last kneading and before the last rise just before the bake cycle starts. There's no need to pause your machine as long as you work quickly and lower the lid within a few minutes.

Step 1: Lift the lid of the machine.

Step 2: Nudge the dough aside or remove the pan from the machine and flip the dough into your hands.

Step 3: Remove the paddle.

Step 4: Reshape the dough into a nice even shape and place it back into the pan.

Step 5: Return the pan to the machine if you removed it.

Step 6: Close the lid and let the machine finish the bake cycle.

NOTE: Some recipes like the Poppy Seed Tea Bread (page 107) and the Lemon Blueberry Bread (page 62) create a very wet mixture that makes removing and reshaping the dough nearly impossible. In these instances, I recommend leaving the paddle in or just gently removing it with the dough in place in the pan.

Why are there dry floury corners on all sides of my bread?

If you have a horizontal bread pan, you may need to help the machine to blend many recipes to avoid this. With the paddle located in the center of the long pan, your machine is likely struggling to catch and blend the ingredients that are pushed into the corners.

During the first kneading cycle, lift the lid of the machine and use a long-handled scraper or spoonula to scrape and push the dry ingredients in the corners toward the growing ball of dough in the center of the machine. Be sure to keep your tool away from the moving paddle itself.

Just scrape down the sides and corners of the bread pan until everything has been absorbed by the dough ball and you're done.

Why didn't my bread rise properly?

The Yeast

The most common cause of a bread failing to rise is the yeast. Be sure you are working with a fresh container of instant yeast. An opened container will expire quickly if it is not stored properly. If you have any doubts, your best bet is to simply start with a fresh container of yeast from the store. You'll find more information on the yeast and how to store it on page 10.

If you're certain your yeast is fresh and active, you may need to be more precise with how you measure your ingredients. Too many extra grams of one ingredient versus another will throw the whole ratio of the dough off. Pay especially close attention to the flour and liquid ingredients—milk, water, juices, etc.—and measure them correctly according to the tips on page 149.

The Flour

If you're measuring by hand with traditional dry ingredient measuring cups, don't overpack your cup. It should have a nice even measure at the top, leveled off with a knife.

Using a food scale to measure the flour is one of the best ways to ensure a perfect loaf every time. Even if you use regular cups and spoons to measure all the other ingredients, weighing the flour will ensure a more perfect ratio for the dough. See page 151 for really easy tips on using an inexpensive food scale.

The Liquid Ingredients

Use a liquid measuring cup and be sure the ingredient is level with the correct marking line on the cup. Place the cup on the counter and bend down to eyeball it at a level height. Better yet, use a food scale to weigh your liquids right in the bread pan itself. Each recipe features the ingredients in both volume and weight to help you achieve accuracy.

The Order of the Ingredients in the Pan

Did you add the ingredients in exactly the order they are listed in the recipe? If you swapped the order, whether intentionally or by accident, the dough may not have blended properly. Pay particular attention so that the salt and yeast are not touching. I like to add the salt to the corners or perimeter of the pan and make a well in the center of the flour for the yeast. See page 13 for more instructions on how to add ingredients to your pan.

Why are all my nuts and raisins stuck on the bottom of my loaf?

Not all bread machines are equal when it comes to blending in the mix-ins. If the recipe calls for especially hearty ingredients like chopped nuts, raisins or dried fruits, you may need to give your machine a slight helping hand.

Near the end the first kneading phase, after you added the mix-ins, take a peek inside the machine. If the ingredients are not mixed in well, it is OK to lift the lid, remove the dough and mix-ins and knead them in by hand. As long as you work swiftly, there's no reason to pause your machine. You can also remove the paddle and reshape the loaf at this time and simply let the machine finish the last rise and bake cycles. For more information on your machine's cycles, see below.

YOU ARE SMARTER THAN YOUR MACHINE

For my first several years of bread machine baking, I assumed something mysterious happened when I closed the lid and pressed Start. I was convinced I would screw everything up if I touched anything before the bread was completely done baking.

After fifteen years of bread baking, I now know that the most delicious breads to come out of your bread machine are the ones where you take a little ownership of the process.

Once you understand the baking cycles of your machine, you'll know just when to step in and interrupt the process to troubleshoot, enhance with tasty swirls and mix-ins, reshape the dough and ensure that the bread turns out exactly as you want it to.

Understanding the Basic Cycles Featured on All Bread Machines

First Knead: This is the first step when the machine briefly blends all the ingredients and forms a rough dough ball. Take a peek; did everything from the corners get blended into the dough ball? If not, lift the lid and scrape down the sides and corners while the paddle works.

Second Knead and Mix-In Additions: This is the stage where the mix-ins are added. By the end of this cycle, if the mix-ins are not evenly distributed or you see some loose in the bottom of the pan, you can remove the dough and knead the ingredients in quickly by hand and return the dough to the machine. If your recipe doesn't call for mix-ins, the machine will simply finish the second knead and continue with the program cycles.

First Rise: This is a quiet time for the dough to settle and the yeast to begin to do its work. By the end of this cycle, you should notice the dough becoming distinctly smoother and puffier.

First Punch: There will be a brief activation of the paddle to "punch down" the dough so that it doesn't overrise in your pan. This also breaks up the air bubbles that are getting between the yeast and their food, allowing them to get back to work.

Second Rise: After the punch down, the dough will rest and rise again. The yeast is now reactivated from the punch down and will continue to add air to your bread, which makes it light and fluffy.

Second Punch and Removing the Paddle: After another brief activation of the paddle, the dough will move into the final phase before baking. Now is the time to remove the paddle from the bread pan if you wish. This is also the phase where you can have a little fun reshaping the dough to make a pull-apart bread or adding a streusel swirl. If you've selected the Dough program, your machine will end at this phase and you will do the final rise on your counter before baking in the oven.

Third Rise: This is the final time for the dough to rise and the yeast to work its magic. You will not want to touch or move the dough during or after this phase or it will affect the final height, texture and shape of your bread.

Bake: The bread machine will bake your bread for just the right amount of time based on the baking program you set at the beginning.

THE ESSENTIAL WAY TO ADD INGREDIENTS TO YOUR BREAD PAN

Remove the bread pan from the bread machine when you are ready to add the ingredients.

Ensure your bread pan is fitted with the paddle before you begin. This will be very difficult to correct once you add the ingredients.

In order for your machine to properly blend everything together and form a perfect dough with that tiny paddle, you need to add the ingredients to the bread pan in a very specific order.

The layers of ingredients will always follow this pattern:

Liquid Ingredients: The milk, water, juices, syrups, oils and/or extracts always go in the bottom of the pan first.

Eggs and Softened Butter: These will be added to the liquids already in the pan so they can be blended in easily. Be sure to cut your softened butter into smaller cubes and sprinkle them around the bottom of the pan so the machine doesn't have to work too hard to blend them in.

Soft or Shredded Cheeses and Raw Fruits and Vegetables: Some recipes will call for these to be added before the flour since they will add liquid to the dough as they warm during the rise cycles. Be sure to shred or dice them as stated in the recipe.

Flour: Just spoon the flour right in on top of the liquids. It will eventually cover them completely.

Sugar, Spices, Herbs and Seasonings: These can be sprinkled right on top of the flour.

Salt: This is the one ingredient to really watch when adding it to the pan. It is crucial to keep the salt and yeast from touching one another before the machine blends them in together. Add the salt to the corners or the perimeter of the pan, avoiding the center of the flour.

Yeast: The yeast is the last ingredient to be added to the pan for the initial mix. In order to keep it away from the salt, use the back of a spoon to form a small well in the top center of the flour and add the yeast to the well.

Mix-Ins: Chopped nuts, raisins, dried fruits and chocolate chips are not added to the dough until the second kneading cycle. If you add them right away, the dough will not blend properly and you will risk having a bread that doesn't rise correctly. Prepare and measure these ingredients and add them to your machine's mix-in dispenser or place them in a small bowl next to the machine so they are ready to go at just the right time.

HOW TO USE A FOOD SCALE TO MAKE PERFECTLY CONSISTENT BREADS EVERY TIME

You bought a bread machine for easy hands-off bread baking. You want to dump and go, not fuss around with a scale and measuring. I totally get it.

But, listen. A plain-Jane, no-frills food scale will cost you less than twenty dollars and save you a lot more than that in the expense of wasted ingredients in failed breads. But perhaps even more importantly, I pinkie swear that it will actually save you time and dirty dishes.

If you plan to experiment with the sourdough recipes on pages 33 and 34, you'll find that a food scale is nearly essential.

Easy Tricks for Using a Food Scale

Place the empty bread pan fitted with the paddle attachment onto your food scale.

Power the food scale on. Most models will now read "0 g," but if your scale is weighing the pan, press the button that says "Tare." It will zero out your scale.

Add the required liquids to the pan until it reads the proper weight. Zero out the scale again.

Add the eggs, butter and any required soft cheeses or fruits and veggies. Zero out the scale between each ingredient if you want to use the scale to weigh it instead of measuring with traditional cups and spoons.

Use a spoon to scoop and add the flour to your pan until the scale reads the correct weight. If you go over, it's OK to collect some of the clean dry flour from the top with your spoon. Zero out the scale.

Add and weigh the sugar, spices, salt and yeast, zeroing out the scale between each one. For especially small ingredients—1 teaspoon or less—I prefer using my measuring spoons but the weight has been provided to offer you that option.

By measuring your ingredients directly in the bread pan on a food scale, you save yourself from needing to wash extra bowls and measuring cups and at the same time ensure a more perfect ratio of liquid to flour for your dough.

HOW TO ASSEMBLE A LAYERED DOUGH IN YOUR BREAD MACHINE

Do you want to make a bread with a flavored swirl right in your bread machine? The Apple Crisp Bread (page 71), Blueberry Streusel Muffin Bread (page 69) and Everything Bagel Bread (page 30) all use the same dough and filling technique. There's no need to overthink this step. Simply have fun adding balls of dough with your favorite flavor sprinkles in the bread pan and enjoy the creation that comes out. See the next page for step by step instructions.

Add the divided portions of dough across the bottom of the bread pan.

Sprinkle the streusel or seasoned filling over the top.

Add a few more pieces of dough and another sprinkle of streusel or seasoning; repeat until all the dough is used.

Sprinkle the top with all the remaining streusel or seasoning.

GETTING STARTED WITH SOURDOUGH

I recommend saving the sourdough recipes for after you're more familiar with your machine. Once you're ready to branch out, sourdough will bring a whole new level of fun to baking with your bread machine.

What is sourdough starter?

This core ingredient for all sourdough breads is a mixture of flour and water that has gathered yeast from the environment all around you over the course of many days. It is used to raise breads without commercial yeast and gives sourdough bread that familiar sour flavor.

Where can I get sourdough starter?

You can make your own from scratch, but it is a many-days long process. The faster route, and the one my family chose, was to simply purchase a container of sourdough starter online from King Arthur Baking. Alternatively, you can get sourdough starter from a friend that has some on hand or check with your local bakeries to see if they sell portions of starter for home bakers.

If you order from King Arthur, a small portion of ready-to-feed starter will arrive in the mail. You feed it simply with water and unbleached all-purpose flour to help it grow in quantity. Be sure to use unbleached flour because bleached flour doesn't have what the sourdough starter needs to eat.

Wait, I have to FEED the starter?

Yes. Your new starter is a living thing, a little like a new houseplant. We named ours Audrey Two. "Feed me, Seymour!"

Simply add unbleached all-purpose flour and water to the starter in a 1:1:1 ratio by weight like this:

- 100 g of all-purpose flour
- 100 g of water
- 100 g of sourdough starter

You'll find a food scale greatly helps this process. For tips on using a food scale, see page 151.

Stir everything together and let it sit in a covered container on your counter until it is bubbly and active. Then, you can use the active starter in a recipe.

When you notice that the starter has "deflated," it's usually time to feed it again to keep it active and healthy. When stored on the counter at room temperature, feed it every day. If your home is very warm, such as during the summer months, you may need to feed it twice a day.

For most people, it's best to store the starter in the fridge in between uses. In this case, your starter goes "dormant" and only needs to be taken out for a feeding once a week. See page 154 for tips on using the fridge to deepen the sour flavor of your starter.

Keep an open mind and watch how your starter behaves over the course of a few weeks; soon you will find a nice rhythm for the feedings that works well for you.

How do I use the starter?

A classic sourdough loaf like the one on page 33 calls for 2 cups (400 g) of sourdough starter; the sourdough dinner buns—my husband's favorite recipe in this whole book—on page 137 only need ½ cup (100 g).

You'll want to measure what you need for the recipe but be sure to save at least ½ cup or 100 grams of starter to feed and maintain so you can bake with it again.

Why do bread machine recipes for sourdough require yeast?

Though sourdough is traditionally used for raising loaves without additional yeast, the process requires very long wait times. To help you get a delicious sourdough bread to the table in hours instead of days, we add a bit of yeast to ensure a solid rise.

I tried the recipe but it didn't taste very sour. What did I do wrong?

Welcome to the fun of from-scratch baking. You didn't do anything wrong—sourdough is a unique ingredient that will make your loaves taste slightly different from bread to bread. Depending on how active your starter is, how long it has hung out in the fridge or how old it is, your breads will range in that sour flavor.

To maximize the sour flavor, measure the starter you need for your recipe and store it in a container in your fridge for at least two to three days or up to a week. Use it directly in your recipe without feeding it and you'll find the bread has a much stronger flavor. Since we're relying on yeast for the rise, you don't have to worry as much about the starter being active.

HOW TO STORE YOUR FRESH BREAD SO THAT IT LASTS LONGER

Bread machine recipes featuring streusel, sweet mix-ins or specialty toppings are generally best the day they are baked. The more basic recipes that do not feature mix-ins will have a three-day lifespan with proper storage.

In a pinch, you can store the completely cooled, room temperature, unsliced bread in an airtight plastic ziplock bag. However, this can lead to a loss in texture.

Old-fashioned bread boxes let you store unsliced fresh bread at room temperature with less harmful waste. The texture of bread stored in a bread box is far better than the plastic bag method but will still result in a slightly softer crust the next day.

If you want to share your newfound baking prowess with friends and family, you may want to consider individual bread bags with twist ties. You can easily find various sizes and shapes of bread bags for sale online.

For longer storage, I recommend slicing your entire loaf and storing it in the freezer in a double-layer bread bag twisted closed. This lets you thaw and use just a slice or two at a time for toast or sandwiches.

MAKE-AHEAD TIPS FOR FITTING HOMEMADE BREAD INTO YOUR BUSY SCHEDULE

Warm, fresh bread perfectly timed with your meal isn't always a viable option. Especially during the busy holiday season, you may need to bake your loaf ahead of time. You can make your machine work for you and use your freezer to extend the life of your baked breads.

Your desired timing, serving plan and recipe will determine which of these options work best.

Option 1: Time your meal and count backward.

Plan to put the ingredients into your bread machine and start the program approximately 4 hours before you plan to serve your meal. Double check with your machine about the duration of the required settings. This will give you warm fresh bread right at the start of your meal.

Works Best For: Regular loaves of bread at dinnertime.

Option 2: Bake it in the morning and store on your countertop.

Bake your bread completely first thing in the morning. Remove it from the bread pan and let it cool on a wire rack. It can stay on the counter until dinnertime and retain its texture as long as you don't slice it.

Works Best For: Really busy days when you want the work out of the way so you can relax in the evening.

Option 3: Make the entire bread the night before and store it properly.

If you want to have a fresh breakfast bread and don't want to set your alarm for three o'clock in the morning, you can bake the bread later in the afternoon or early evening of the day before. To refresh the bread, you can place it on a baking sheet and warm it in your regular oven at 300°F (149°C) for 5 minutes.

Works Best For: Sweet breads for breakfast or brunch and most dinner rolls that will be reheated gently before serving.

Option 4: Bake the entire recipe ahead of time and freeze.

Cool your bread completely, store it unsliced in an airtight container and freeze it for up to three months. Remove it from the freezer the day before you want to enjoy it and place it on the counter overnight with the packaging seal cracked open to allow a little bit of airflow. This will prevent the bread from becoming soggy due to condensation inside the packaging. To refresh it, simply place it on a baking sheet and warm it in your regular oven at 300°F (149°C) for 5 minutes.

Works Best For: Simple sandwich-style loaves without fancy toppings, dinner rolls and for busy families that love to batch-prep foods for busy seasons.

Option 5: Make the dough the night before and bake fresh in the morning.

For many of the shaped breads in Chapter 5 (page 111), you can prepare the dough the day before, shape your desired rolls and cover the pan tightly in plastic wrap for storing in the fridge overnight.

In the morning, place the pan on your counter, loosen the plastic wrap and allow the dough to do the final rise before baking. You may need a little more time for the rise as the dough needs to come to room temperature before the yeast really gets to work.

Works Best For: Cinnamon rolls and dinner rolls.

THANK YOUS & ACKNOWLEDGMENTS

I usually save the best for last, but if it weren't for my husband Tim's total excitement and enthusiasm for this project, this lovely book wouldn't exist. He was there even before the very start and held my hand right through to the finish. Sweetie, I couldn't have done this without you and I'm thrilled we've found something we both love to do in the kitchen together.

If it weren't for my amazing editor Sarah Monroe's suggestion that we play around with bread machine recipes, my family's deep love of bread may never have seen the light of day. Sarah, thank you so much for the inspiration and the passion you brought to this project. You and the entire team at Page Street helped create a book straight out of my dreams.

I wish everyone could be as blessed and lucky as I am to be surrounded by passionate friends. Hearty thanks go to Zina and Nya Harrington for using their love of home baking to give me a real-world check-in on the flavor lineup and cheering this book on from the start. Michelle Malek's love of entertaining and feeding her friends inspired me with many of the serving suggestions. Jennifer Carter Radinsky's love of her chickens filled my basket with gorgeous farm-fresh eggs for recipe testing. And as always, Carey Pace's love for light and color helped inspire me for the photos. Ladies, thank you so much for being my creative tribe.

Thank you to my mother-in-law, Evelyn Dahle, for giving us our first bread machine as an unexpected surprise gift many, many Christmases ago. None of us could have guessed what would come from that thoughtful gift.

And to my sweet girls, Sophie and Charlotte, thank you for everything you did to help our family create this amazing "quarantine project." I hope we'll always remember how awesome it was to be together every single day, testing recipes and working together. Everything I bake tastes better when I'm sharing it with you.

Lastly, thank you to each and every reader of Peanut Blossom. I firmly believe you are the kindest community on the Internet and I'm the luckiest girl when I get to connect with you. I'm beyond honored that you choose to make my recipes a part of your family.

ABOUT THE AUTHOR

As a little girl, Tiffany Dahle always dreamed of owning an Easy Bake Oven. She is utterly convinced her bread machine is the next best thing.

Tiffany believes the kitchen is the best place to play with her kids and is the author of two best-selling cookbooks for families. Her popular blog, Peanut Blossom, helps busy parents cook kid-friendly recipes that adults will actually enjoy while finding something fun to celebrate about each day of the year. You can find her work in *Better Homes & Gardens*, *Good Housekeeping*, *Taste of Home*, *Country Living*, *Woman's Day*, Tasty and BuzzFeed.

INDEX

A

almond butter
 Almond Cherry Bread, 82
almond extract
 Almond Cherry Bread, 82
 Chocolate Almond Bread, 77–78
Aloha Pineapple Bread, 75–76
Amaretto
 Spiced Eggnog & Pear Bread, 92
apples and apple juice
 Apple Crisp Bread, 71–72

B

baby food, sweet potato
 Savory Sweet Potato Bread, 44
bacon
 Loaded Baked Potato Bread, 51
Bagel Bread, Everything, 30
bananas
 Best Banana Bread, The, 65
 Classic Hummingbird Bread, 101–102
Beer Flight Bread, The, 55
bell peppers
 Farmers' Market Veggie Patch Bread, 40
Best Banana Bread, The, 65
blue cheese
 Honeyed Blue Cheese Bread, 52
blueberries
 Blueberry Streusel Muffin Bread, 69–70
 Lemon Blueberry Bread, 62

bread machines
 assembling layered dough in, 151
 basic cycles of, 149–150
 convenient timing of baking, 154–155
 flour on corners of loaf from, 147
 flours for, 145
 kinds of breads made by, 145
 making dough in, 112–114, 145
 mix-ins and, 149, 150
 order of adding ingredients to, 13, 149, 150–151
 paddle and its removal, 10, 147, 149, 150
 proper rising of bread, 147, 149
 quick start guide to, 10–11, 13
 removing loaf from, 13
 size and shape of loaves from, 10, 146
Brioche, 61
Brown Bread, Steakhouse, 29
brown sugar
 Blueberry Streusel Muffin Bread, 69–70
 Brown Sugar Oatmeal Bread, 18
 Buttery Dinner Rolls, 118
 Caramel Pecan Breakfast Buns, 141, 143
 Caraway Rye Bread, 26
 Classic Cinnamon Rolls, 123–124
 Classic Pretzel Twists, 128, 130–132
 Fluffy Focaccia, 127
 Hot Buttered Rum Bread, 88
 Sun-Dried Tomato Parmesan Bread, 48
Buttered Rum Glaze, 88
buttermilk
 Classic Hummingbird Bread, 101–102
 Lemon Blueberry Bread, 62
 Luck of the Irish Soda Bread, 108

buttermilk powder
    Hot Cross Buns, 115, 117
    Maple Pecan Bread, 66
Buttery Dinner Rolls, 118

C

candied pineapple
    Aloha Pineapple Bread, 75–76
Caramel Pecan Breakfast Buns, 141, 143
caraway seeds
    Caraway Rye Bread, 26
    Savory Swiss & Onion Bread, 43
carrots
    Farmers' Market Veggie Patch Bread, 40
    Sweet Carrot Cake Bread, 103–104
cheddar cheese
    Jalapeño Popper Cornbread, 56
    Loaded Baked Potato Bread, 51
cherries, dried
    Almond Cherry Bread, 82
chives
    Loaded Baked Potato Bread, 51
Chocolate Almond Bread, 77–78
chocolate chips. *See* semisweet chocolate chips;
   white chocolate chips
cinnamon
    Apple Crisp Bread, 71–72
    Best Banana Bread, The, 65
    Blueberry Streusel Muffin Bread, 69
    Cinnamon Orange Pretzels, 134
    Cinnamon Raisin Bread, 22
    Classic Cinnamon Rolls, 123–124
    Classic Hummingbird Bread, 101–102
    Hot Buttered Rum Bread, 88
    Hot Cross Buns, 115, 117

It's Not a Fruitcake Bread, 97–98
    Orange Chocolate Chip Bread, 81
    Sweet Carrot Cake Bread, 103–104
Classic Pretzel Twists, 128, 130–132
cloves
    Hot Buttered Rum Bread, 88
    It's Not a Fruitcake Bread, 97–98
cocoa powder
    Chocolate Almond Bread, 77–78
    Steakhouse Brown Bread, 29
coconut
    Aloha Pineapple Bread, 75–76
Cornbread, Jalapeño Popper, 56
Cranberry & White Chocolate Delight, 95–96
Cranberry Spice Pretzels, 134
cream cheese
    Cream Cheese Frosting, 138, 140
    Cream Cheese Glaze, 101, 103
    Strawberry Cream Cheese Swirls, 140
Cucumber Dill Tzatziki Bread, 47
currants
    Hot Cross Buns, 115, 117
    Luck of the Irish Soda Bread, 108

D

dill
    Cucumber Dill Tzatziki Bread, 47
Dinner Rolls, Buttery, 118
dough. *See also* sourdough starter
    assembling layered dough, 151
    making in machine but baking in oven, 112–114, 145

E

eggnog
    Spiced Eggnog & Pear Bread, 92
eggs
    Aloha Pineapple Bread, 75–76
    Apple Crisp Bread, 71–72
    Best Banana Bread, The, 65
    Blueberry Streusel Muffin Bread, 69–70
    Brioche, 61
    Buttery Dinner Rolls, 118
    Caramel Pecan Breakfast Buns, 141, 143
    Chocolate Almond Bread, 77–78
    Cranberry & White Chocolate Delight, 95–96
    Everything Bagel Bread, 30
    Garlic Pull-Apart Bread, 121–122
    Honey Whole Wheat Bread, 21
    Hot Cross Buns, 115, 117
    Italian Bread, 25
    It's Not a Fruitcake Bread, 97–98
    Luck of the Irish Soda Bread, 108
    Orange Chocolate Chip Bread, 81
    Poppy Seed Tea Bread, 107
    Savory Swiss & Onion Bread, 43
    Sweet Carrot Cake Bread, 103–104
    Warm & Cozy Pumpkin Bread, 87
English cucumber
    Cucumber Dill Tzatziki Bread, 47
Epic Party Pretzel Platter, 133–134
espresso powder
    Chocolate Almond Bread, 77–78
Everything Bagel Bread, 30

F

Farmers' Market Veggie Patch Bread, 40
flour
    order of adding ingredients and, 150
    rising of bread and, 149
    storing of, 145
Focaccia, Fluffy, 127
food scales, measuring of ingredients and, 151
fruits, dried. *See also specific fruits*
    It's Not a Fruitcake Bread, 97–98

G

Garlic Pull-Apart Bread, 121–122
ginger
    It's Not a Fruitcake Bread, 97–98
glazes, icings and frostings
    Buttered Rum Glaze, Hot, 88
    Classic Cinnamon Rolls, 123–124
    Cream Cheese Frosting, 138, 140
    Cream Cheese Glaze, 101, 103
    Vanilla Glaze, 115
green onions
    Farmers' Market Veggie Patch Bread, 40
    Savory Sweet Potato Bread, 44

H

honey
    Cinnamon Raisin Bread, 22
    Honey Sriracha Pretzels, 134
    Honey Whole Wheat Bread, 21
    Honeyed Blue Cheese Bread, 52
    Milk & Honey Bread, 17
    Steakhouse Brown Bread, 29

Hot Buttered Rum Bread, 88
Hot Cross Buns, 115, 117
Hummingbird Bread, Classic, 101–102

I

Irish Soda Bread, Luck of the, 108
Italian Bread, 25
Italian herb blend
    Garlic Pull-Apart Bread, 121–122
    Sourdough Pesto Swirl, 34
    Sun-Dried Tomato Parmesan Bread, 48
It's Not a Fruitcake Bread, 97–98

J

Jalapeño Popper Cornbread, 56
Jalapeño Poppy Seed Pretzels, 134

K

King Arthur Baking, 145, 153

L

lemon juice and lemon zest
    Lemon Blueberry Bread, 62
    Poppy Seed Tea Bread, 107
liquid ingredients
    order of adding ingredients, 150
    rising of bread and, 149
Loaded Baked Potato Bread, 51
Luck of the Irish Soda Bread, 108

M

maple syrup
    Caramel Pecan Breakfast Buns, 141, 143
    Maple Pecan Bread, 66
mashed potatoes
    Loaded Baked Potato Bread, 51
Milk & Honey Bread, 17
molasses
    Steakhouse Brown Bread, 29
Muffin Bread, Blueberry Streusel, 69–70

N

nutmeg
    Blueberry Streusel Muffin Bread, 69–70
    Hot Buttered Rum Bread, 88
    It's Not a Fruitcake Bread, 97–98
    Spiced Eggnog & Pear Bread, 92
nuts
    Best Banana Bread, The, 65
    Caramel Pecan Breakfast Buns, 141, 143
    Classic Hummingbird Bread, 101–102
    It's Not a Fruitcake Bread, 97–98
    Maple Pecan Bread, 66

O

oats
    Brown Sugar Oatmeal Bread, 18
olive oil
    Beer Flight Bread, 55
    Jalapeño Popper Cornbread, 56
    Rosemary Herb Bread, 39
onions
    Savory Stuffing Bread, 91
    Savory Swiss & Onion Bread, 43

orange juice and orange zest
  Blueberry Streusel Muffin Bread, 69–70
  Luck of the Irish Soda Bread, 108
  Orange Chocolate Chip Bread, 81
oregano
  Jalapeño Popper Cornbread, 56
  Rosemary Herb Bread, 39

P

Parmesan cheese
  Garlic Pull-Apart Bread, 121–122
  Sun-Dried Tomato Parmesan Bread, 48
pears
  Spiced Eggnog & Pear Bread, 92
pecans
  Best Banana Bread, The, 65
  Caramel Pecan Breakfast Buns, 141, 143
  Classic Hummingbird Bread, 101–102
  Maple Pecan Bread, 66
pesto
  Sourdough Pesto Swirl, 34
pineapple and pineapple juice
  Aloha Pineapple Bread, 75–76
  Classic Hummingbird Bread, 101–102
  Sweet Carrot Cake Bread, 103–104
Poppy Seed Tea Bread, 107
potatoes
  Loaded Baked Potato Bread, 51
poultry seasoning
  Savory Stuffing Bread, 91
powdered sugar
  Buttered Rum Glaze, 88
  Classic Cinnamon Roll icing, 123–124
  Cream Cheese Frosting, 138, 140
  Cream Cheese Glaze, 101, 103
  Vanilla Glaze, 115, 117

Pretzel Platter, Epic Party, 133–134
Pretzel Twists, Classic, 128, 130–132
Pull-Apart Bread, Garlic, 121–122
pumpkin puree
  Warm & Cozy Pumpkin Bread, 87
pumpkin spice
  Pumpkin Spice Pretzels, 134
  Warm & Cozy Pumpkin Bread, 87

R

Raisin Bread, Cinnamon, 22
red pepper flakes
  Garlic Pull-Apart Bread, 121–122
Rolls, Buttery Dinner, 118
Rosemary Herb Bread, 39
rum
  Hot Buttered Rum Bread, 88
rye flour
  Caraway Rye Bread, 26

S

Savory Stuffing Bread, 91
Savory Sweet Potato Bread, 44
Savory Swiss & Onion Bread, 43
semisweet chocolate chips
  Chocolate Almond Bread, 77–78
  Orange Chocolate Chip Bread, 81
sour cream
  Cucumber Dill Tzatziki Bread, 47
  Lemon Blueberry Bread, 62
  Poppy Seed Tea Bread, 107
sourdough starter
  basics of starting and feeding, 153–154
  Sourdough Pesto Swirl, 34

Speedy Sourdough Loaf, 33
Tim's Buns, 137
Speedy Sourdough Loaf, 33
Spiced Eggnog & Pear Bread, 92
Steakhouse Brown Bread, 29
storage
of baked bread, 154
of bread flour, 145
Strawberry Cream Cheese Swirls, 138, 140
Streusel Topping, 69–70
Stuffing Bread, Savory, 91
Sun-Dried Tomato Parmesan Bread, 48
Sweet Carrot Cake Bread, 103–104
Sweet Potato Bread, Savory, 44
Swiss cheese
Savory Swiss & Onion Bread, 43

T

Tea Bread, Poppy Seed, 107
thyme
Farmers' Market Veggie Patch Bread, 40
Honeyed Blue Cheese Bread, 52
Savory Sweet Potato Bread, 44
Tim's Buns, 137
tomato sauce
Sun-Dried Tomato Parmesan Bread, 48
Tzatziki Bread, Cucumber Dill, 47

V

vanilla
Classic Cinnamon Rolls, 123–124
Classic Hummingbird Bread, 101–102
Cranberry & White Chocolate Delight, 95–96
Strawberry Cream Cheese Swirls, 138, 140
Sweet Carrot Cake Bread, 103–104

W

Warm & Cozy Pumpkin Bread, 87
white chocolate chips
Cranberry & White Chocolate Delight, 95–96
whole wheat flour
Cinnamon Raisin Bread, 22
Honey Whole Wheat Bread, 21
Savory Swiss & Onion Bread, 43
Steakhouse Brown Bread, 29
Sun-Dried Tomato Parmesan Bread, 48

Y

yeast
rising of bread and, 10, 147
sourdough and, 154

Z

zucchini
Farmers' Market Veggie Patch Bread, 40